Praise for *I'm Sor*

M000317943

Dr. Janet Bieschke has written a book that will offer something to every reader. There are antidotes and lessons that are helpful for those who are experiencing the impending loss of a loved-one. One such teaching is the concept of appreciation during a time when someone you care about is dying. It is an important paradox not often expressed. I recommend this book as it is written in an authentic style – full of hope and compassion.

- Dr. Laura Hyatt, Professor, University of La Verne

You are holding an invaluable, compassionate, and healing intimate journey into life, death, and the cherished memories that can be created for a lifetime. Dr. Janet Bieschke has graciously given us the gift of sharing her gifts and deep insights with us. This book powerfully guides us through those last tender moments with our loved ones and offers us an affirming message of hope and healing.

- Evelyn Apostolou, Founder,
Quantum Edge Healing Institute

How I wish I had this divinely transformational book to guide me, soothe me, educate me and allow me the closure that everyone hopes for when a loved one dies. As a former dancer with the James Brown Revue, I have traveled the world and seen and experienced the dynamic and powerful ability of people as they connect emotions and actions of love. Janet's book possesses that same universal and divine connection of people as they express their emotions and actions of love.

- Lola! Love, LOAcc, DTM

Janet showcases her wisdom, engaging stories and spiritual principles to assist families in facing their end of life experience. I loved the valuable understanding and tools provided, like *Letters for Later* that we can use immediately. This is truly a gift to provide comfort in the time of need. Thank you, Janet.

- Cathy Brown, Master Law of Attraction Life Coach,
https://lifecoachingbycathy.com/

Dr. Janet Bieschke's chosen life path, and now this book she has written, is a blessing to all of us who are fortunate enough to find her and her work. Thank you, Dr. Janet. I will be forever grateful.

- Kelly McKinstry

I'm Sorry, I Love You, Goodbye

Harvesting the sacred gifts of the final days

DR. JANET M. BIESCHKE

I'm Sorry, I Love You, Goodbye

Harvesting the sacred gifts of the final days

 Capucia

Published by:
Capucia, LLC
211 Pauline Drive #513
York, PA 17402
www.capuciapublishing.com

ISBN: 978-1-945252-42-6
Library of Congress Control Number: 2018955989

Cover Design: Ranilo Cabo
Layout: Ranilo Cabo
Editor and Proofreader: Simon Whaley
Book Midwife: Carrie Jareed

Printed in the United States of America

Dedication

I dedicate this book to my sister Theresa, who reminds me
that death doesn't wait until we are ready.

Foreword by Christy Whitman

If you find yourself in the midst of the pain of an impending loss; if you are struggling about what to do or say; with how to process the wide range of emotions you are feeling; or wondering how to make the most of the precious time you have left with a loved one, take heart, because you have been guided to the perfect place.

I met Dr. Janet Bieschke in the fall of 2008, when she was among the very first group of students to graduate from the yearlong Law of Attraction coach certification program that I facilitate twice a year through my Quantum Success Coaching Academy. From my earliest interactions with Janet, I came to appreciate the question that naturally seemed to bubble up within her after devouring each of the sequentially deepening coaching programs that I offer: "What's next?"

Janet has been on an enlightened energy path for many years, and – as you are soon to discover – she is a humble, confident, caring woman with a sweet sense of humor and a huge contribution to make. In this book, she draws from that deep well of wisdom, compassion, and spiritual insight.

This important work was inspired through Janet as the result of ten years of mindful, soulful and heart-opening experiences that unfolded during her many interactions with hospice patients, elders, and their families. In it, she brings together a wealth of resources, practices and insights – all field-tested from her own experiences – to help all who are coming to terms with the impending death of a loved one. A powerful message awaits the reader on these pages, for, in embracing its wisdom, the prospect of losing a loved one will surely lose a little more of its sting.

Christy Whitman
Scottsdale, AZ
Spring, 2018

Table of Contents

Introduction

Thank you for reading this book. Though it will be helpful as a guide to anyone facing a major shift in life, I write it to those of you about to lose a parent or a close loved one. If you have just stepped back into your parent's world as a caregiver or to bring support, it may be daunting for you to realize how emotionally challenging this period will become.

I write with you in mind, knowing that your life is about to take some changes that you may not have yet anticipated. You already know the impending changes will bring a degree of loss. And, regardless of who it is that may be leaving your life, it's common that your first thoughts encompass what you are losing, who you are losing, what may change, and how things will change. You are not alone.

After retiring from my postal career of 34 years, I trained to work for a hospice organization. My volunteering began in personal and respite care. Then approximately ten years ago, an unusual opportunity was created by a patient who wanted to find a way to ease the pain of loss being expressed by his friend who didn't want to let him go. Initially he thought it would help to write a loving goodbye letter to the friend. Somehow, that shifted, and I used a video camera to record the goodbye message. In the process, the goodbye message expanded, and the video became a collection of his earliest memories, wishes, stories, expressions of love, and finally his waving goodbye with a nice big smile on his face. In the process, something wonderful and rewarding happened. I soon interviewed another patient—and another. Then I interviewed the 99-year-old mother of a friend who was in a nursing home. The interviewing took on a life of its own and each one brought new knowledge and insights about the final days.

During this same decade, my mother had a stroke and declined, as dementia slowly and consistently took her away from us. That's another story. As more people learned what I was doing, I heard, "I only wish we would have known about the work you are doing when my Mother/Father was still alive." Sadly, I could say the same. So, what you have in your hands is a by-product of tools and things I wish I'd known earlier.

Though these are challenging times, little decisions can make big differences, and there are many ways of creating memories, happy times, and lightness as you journey forward. Be gentle with yourself. Please use this book as a simple, effective tool to guide you through the journey so you also understand that, when a life ends, the final and most precious gifts available to any of us will come in the form of peace, healing and closure.

This book provides many tools needed to walk through the tough questions. You and your loved one will find special connections and pleasure in completing the Letters For Later and the Notes For Now. I only wish they had been available for me to use when I sat in the hospital with my father, following his heart attack, and we both felt the awkward silence between us. Some parents did all they could to raise children without expressing many emotions. In those situations, it is helpful to have a framework to open up meaningful conversations. With that in mind, I've also included the Five Easy Conversation Starters template as a place to begin. I've used these tools and found them great for friends and family when conversations are otherwise uncomfortable.

My hope for everyone venturing into this territory is that, during the upcoming critical days, you take actions that are nurturing and helpful to bring a most peaceful, if not joyful, passing to your loved one. What's possible to do now is to harvest the gifts of the final days. And in doing so, to receive the gift of knowing you can create positive choices for your loved one. This is a time to give loved ones hope, peace, satisfaction, the knowledge that their life mattered and they made a difference. This is the work where we can choose to show up in the valuable role serving as a difference maker.

Though I do not personally know you, I know many in similar situations. I've experienced the challenges and have witnessed issues that arise as lives enter the final days. It does not matter whether it is a medical condition or just age that brings us here. Certain things are predictable, and others will throw us for a loop because each death is unique and can impact us in unexpected ways. Even when the health and legal paperwork is completed, we may avoid discussing the issues that impact the soul, that carry the spirit and hold the memories. Who could have prepared us for them? How do we help another heal their own wounds and bring closure to issues that have been suppressed for a lifetime? Fortunately, I have found ways that seem to work quite well. You will find them in the pages to come. It's easier to absorb loss through the experiences of others. It's quite different when it gets personal. Sometimes we don't even have an adequate answer when someone notices our pain and asks the question, "How are you doing?"

Many of us experience a feeling of emptiness during this time and become acutely aware of the missed opportunities, as planned activities or dreams fade away because it's now *too late*. What I imagine is true about you is that in your best days, you're accepting things as they come, you are finding peace, you're saying what you need to say, doing what you need to do, letting go of things that need to be released, and that you're doing a pretty good job of holding it all together. On other days, you may be paralyzed with the responsibility coming your way. It's too easy to find old fears resurfacing, hoping to avoid unnecessary drama, or sensing frustrations as we realize the need to engage with people from our past. It's reasonable to want to minimize the emotional rollercoaster ride as we struggle to make tough family decisions.

I feel as though I am holding both sides of a precious and volatile coin. Throughout a decade of simultaneously coaching and volunteering, I've witnessed a lot and have decided to bring some of the overlapping pieces together in this book. As a certified Law of Attraction Life Coach, I offer clients an ability to totally shift the direction of their lives from areas of struggle to lives they create from love. By doing this, they get to write life stories that are worth remembering and sharing when their time comes. For some, that means shifting from depressed, overweight, feelings of unworthiness, being unloved or unlovable, and being unfocused into all that represents the opposites of those. For others, it means redirecting past choices, relationships, careers, or inner struggles into purpose, meaning, and happiness. For all, it means creating a life filled with many moments of gratitude, joy, permission, and peace.

As a hospice volunteer, I offer my non-judging presence in ways that brings comfort. Most of this time is spent just showing up, sitting with patients, walking with them, listening to them and sharing the space while they come to terms and accept the inevitable changes. For others, who I interview and capture their life stories, I offer the gift of remembrance, history, healing, and closure. This is their time for legacy work. Throughout this book, I share stories to bring topics to light. The beautiful people behind these stories include family, friends, a couple of patients who provided permission to be recorded, and in at least one case, the situation was created from memory. I have received feedback from families adamantly claiming my time spent interviewing their loved one became the turning point to a peaceful passing. That is powerful feedback.

This is not a guide to dying; but, rather a book you may open to any section and begin reading. Stories hold meaning and there are many stories tucked within these pages. The poems are those I'd written after being inspired by someone close to death. For confidentiality, the names and locations have been changed, unless I am referring to one of my family members. These are individual stories, which means they are not always neat and organized. Yet, hopefully within the messiness, you will find a needed, uplifting message that speaks to you and to your specific situation.

SECTION ONE

I'M SORRY

Just Maybe

I could have, you should have; we didn't.
I should, you could; we don't.

The pine trees are swaying from
the cold, driving winds. They are planted
firmly in the frozen, snow-covered ground.

I notice them only because today's
sunshine was glaring strong~
right before she swiftly slipped below the horizon.

I don't want to remember this day
while still holding crazy coulds and shoulds.

You are ready to slip away.
Can either of us take this last chance
to say I'm sorry, I love you, or goodbye before you go?

Just Maybe?

Janet Bieschke

CHAPTER ONE

WHAT TO DO WHEN YOU HEAR "THERE'S NOTHING MORE WE CAN DO"

When and how? That's what most people want to know. Just when will I die, and how will I die? How would our days and lives change if only we had those answers? What risks would we be willing to take today, or this week, knowing it wasn't yet our time? How much better would we care for our bodies if we knew of the many decades remaining for it to serve us? Would we give more attention to nutrition and exercises?

We accept the fact we are going to die, our parents are going to die, and even our children or grandchildren may die before us. This book will be centered on those final days when a parent or loved one receives the knowledge that the time is soon. What to do?

The reaction may be dependent upon whether the final days are coming as a result of the aging process or from cancer, heart failure, leukemia, or a different medical condition. When the final days come because of illness, it can be more traumatic, and the biggest question may be *why*? Why now? Why to me? Why, why, and why?

When it's your aging parent hearing these words from a doctor, it may come to them as a shock. But most likely, they may have been anticipating it for some time. They may have noticed changes in their body and their emotions, or they may have just sensed that something has fundamentally changed. Their intuitions may have already provided this information that their cycle of life is getting closer to the end days. If the final days are coming solely as a result of age, they may have thought about their own death when they lost a friend, a relative, a colleague, or just a close acquaintance.

When we first hear these words, it may totally dump our world upside down. Because even though we may have seen some changes or noticed some differences, our mind may have protected us by going into denial. Our mind may begin swimming with questions, with some denial, with hope that the diagnosis is wrong, or just filled with all the things that we still want to do while our parent is still alive.

This is a time when we, as the adult child, may be pulled back into our parent's world and all it entails. If we live close to them, it may be more natural to integrate our daily schedule into theirs. We may be acquainted with their doctor, the clinic they use, the church they attend, their friends and neighbors, and possibly even many of their financial routines. But this is not necessarily true. As an adult with our own lifestyle, friends, career, and possibly separation by choice, we may be physically close and yet emotionally distant.

Either way, the approaching death of a parent has the ability to pull us back home in so many ways. We may learn new things about how our parents have been living. We may find they have everything in order, or nothing in order. This includes their health care directives, their legal documented decisions, their household belongings, their spiritual understandings, and whether or not we agree with their choices. This time may afford us the luxury of engaging into conversations that have been reserved until the necessity of this time makes them mandatory.

Everyone has different emotions and different ways of displaying their emotions. At this time, emotions and how they are handled, can literally make the difference between the final days being terrified, angry, confused, frustrated and vindictive, or respectful, concerned, grieving, engaged, caring, supportive, and meaningful. This is a time when many families are driven apart— never to speak to each other again during their lifetimes, or a time where healing and closure can bring new meaning to old stories and experiences.

In my family, we did a wonderful job of coming together to decide upon healthcare issues, household issues, and disbursement of possessions. And though we didn't have 100% agreement on any of these issues, we agreed enough to work through decisions and to do what needed to be done. When it came to dividing up possessions, everyone was asked to identify three items that they were interested in receiving. Additionally, everyone had to prioritize these three items on their list. When it came time to go through the items, we rotated through the family and beginning with the eldest, a selection was made and the next person would make their choice. We repeated the process again, beginning with the youngest making their next selection. We continued until the majority of the items were disseminated. At some point, it was decided to donate the remaining items to a local thrift shop or to a church.

A key point for our family was that we did this while our mother was still alive and the emotions were not as raw. I think we had more ability to remain rational and logical. In hindsight, I'm quite sure it would not have gone so smoothly had we waited until after her death. This was the situation for our family: your family may require and choose something totally different. There is no right or wrong way to do some of these things.

If and how we choose to react emotionally--along with our levels of engagement--can make all the difference in creating a peaceful passing that holds space for loving, releasing, understanding, and acceptance. This is the time when we can choose to either revert to our old childhood roles or choose to use our adult understanding and come back and witness our parent in new and different ways. The key question is: what is the experience we want to create? And then the biggest answers come in the form of engagement. In coaching, we refer to this as setting a clear intention, knowing that what we chose to focus upon will expand and show up in more areas of our life. The saying is *Like attracts Like*. There are huge opportunities to give and receive some sacred gifts during these final days. They include paying attention to our parent, their emotions, their desires, their hopes and dreams, their values, and their history. Who are they, and what is the identity that makes them exist? These are powerful things to know and will provide keys to creating an exciting experience for us and our parent.

I found a quote by Timothy Bentley in many books, but took this one from a book called Checklist for Life for Teachers: Timeless Wisdom and Foolproof Strategies for Making the Most of Life's Challenges and Opportunities (ISBN: 9780785260028):

"Whenever you're in conflict with someone, there is one factor that can make the difference between damaging your relationship and deepening it. That factor is attitude."

It's important because, in similar situations, the outcomes often are determined by our attitudes. In working with families, it's easy to see how the same situations can be met with completely different behaviors and actions, and, of course, then yielding completely opposite results. I've ruined some opportunities when my attitude was out of alignment, and I've nailed some amazing successes by setting my attitude and holding my focus and following through with determination. When life gets tough, choosing a brighter attitude in thinking can really make a world of difference for everyone involved.

CHAPTER TWO

HEALING WHAT NEEDS TO BE HEALED

Because of the importance of this, and because it's easy to become lost when others seem to be requiring so much from the caregiver, it bears repeating. Healing can occur for many during the time of someone's death. As we hold space for a parent or a loved one, we can benefit from our own healing. It begins with self-care.

Be good to yourself and don't lose yourself in your role of caregiver. Yoga, prayer, meditation, or even just taking a nice long walk in nature are all helpful reflective practices when daily demands begin to take their toll. Schedule regular nutritious meals and if your nights are sleepless, give yourself permission to grab naps during the day. Talking with friends, colleagues, or even professionals who you know and trust also helps to process your thoughts and feelings.

The benefits of gratitude and appreciation are similar in the benefits they hold for the giver and the receiver. Medically, physically, and emotionally, they are proven to improve our overall state of being. When we look for something, we find it. When we make assumptions about others, we notice evidence of our assumptions in the behavior of others. It's said that we can bring out the best in another.

The opposite holds true; we can bring out the worst in others. What we focus on becomes our reality. If that is true, then why wouldn't we choose to think the best, see the best and bring out the best in others? Most likely, it is because we struggle to do that, even when we are dealing with ourselves. Oh, the joys of being human!

Gratitude and appreciation are at the root of almost every piece of happiness we will ever find. They are also wrapped all around our beliefs and behaviors of love. In my opinion and observations, all of these are energetically light emotions, and they are grouped together. Lighter emotions are those that feel good. They feel good and they make others feel good. Joy, happiness, kindness, love, optimism, passion and hopefulness are energetically light emotions. They include empowerment, because each of these emotions allows us to take action that leads us closer to feeling even better. Where you find one, it is most likely the others will be present.

When a person is naturally grateful for their state of being, their circumstances, and the people in their lives, that person is usually predisposed to be appreciative, thankful, happy, kind and loving. I call these people the difference makers.

Conversely, someone who tends to wake up miserable, discontent, worried, angry, insecure, jealous, frustrated, overwhelmed and unappreciative will find many more reasons during the course of their day to believe the world is a cruel place, nothing is working out, and people are out to get him/her. They will likely make it similar for those people unfortunate enough to be living and working around them. I refer to this type of person as the angry victim. Of course, the world will prove each of these people correct.

It is a universal law that 'like attracts like' and thoughts, beliefs, and emotions are so powerful that they hold a magnetic ability to bring results that are aligned and in perfect harmony with them. Whether it is in the Bible, the movie called *The Secret*, Stephen Covey's myriad of teachings, the Laws of Attraction, Appreciative Inquiry findings, or just experiences in our lives, the sayings *Ask and You Shall Receive*; *As You Believe, So Shall You Find*, or *Ask and It Is Given* have proven to be incredibly instrumental as teaching tools.

We notice the boomerang effect of whatever we put out into the universe. I still have days when I need to stop and remember this. Usually, it's after I realize things aren't going well and realize that my attitude stinks. Time out. This is when I ask myself, what do I want? How do I want to feel? It's like hitting my reset buttons.

This can be especially noticeable in people struggling with dementia. As I mentioned earlier, our mother died piece by piece, because of this nasty disease. Our lives turned upside down until we became more knowledgeable of the impact of our emotions and vibrational energy upon her. As an empty container, she absorbed the emotions we brought into her room and then she magnified them and gave them back to us tenfold. If we were anxious, worried, concerned, fearful, upset, or angry, she became filled with the emotions, though she may not have any idea what the issue or the words involved. If we were sad, it filled her. How could that be? Author and nationwide speaker, Jolene Brackey *(www.enhancedmoments.com)* was a godsend in educating us. We purchased her books and DVDs when they were the only helpful resource we could find. The link with more products and services is added in case you are interested in learning how to create moments of joy, even when it doesn't seem that there's much room left for good emotions.

Mom was diagnosed before the healthcare system had a clue how to handle these patients. For ten years, we looked for understanding and knowledge as she slowly gave way to the calls of dementia, a disease that eventually claimed every single fiber of her being.

Fortunately, knowledge became powerful, and we realized this worked in the same manner when our emotions were happy, goofy, playful, laughing and loving. It took focus and lots of practice to remember that regardless of what issues we needed to handle, we needed to *get it together* before walking into her presence. Sometimes we forgot. Too many times we forgot. She and her attitude quickly reminded us and because, by then, she had no short-term memory, her attitudes and emotions bounced back into lighter happier emotions as soon as ours set the stage. Fortunately, she followed suit. Because her long-term memory stayed intact for most of her life, we found prayers to be something that she immediately responded to, and that was fortunate in times when her emotions had no filters.

What I have learned and will share is that these beliefs, thoughts, and feelings are within our choice. If we have been exposed to negativity, we can decide to change and chose differently. That means we can create our life to be based upon our choices. The nice thing about that is that regardless of our family, parents, teachers, friends, partners, co-workers, and bosses who have been a part of our life, we can choose. It may take practice. It may take time. What it really takes is a decision and a commitment. Once we align with that which we want, decide why it is important to us, believe and trust we can have it exactly as we choose, then the actions and behaviors will lead us to the results and outcomes that we know are possible.

So why does this matter? Believe it or not, the habits we form over a lifetime are the same ones we will have as we approach our dying days. That is no surprise, but there are those of us who think we will somehow clean up our life or change drastically when death comes knocking. That's highly unlikely. If we have cultivated gratitude and appreciation, we will reap the benefits of those in our final days. They will affect our attitudes, and they also will impact those who will be caring for us, visiting us, and supporting us and our families.

It isn't difficult to imagine the many issues of conflict that arise when families attempt to resolve finance and business decisions, health decisions, or living arrangements when they are entrenched with guilt, anger, revenge, discouragement, disappointments, worry, and blame. These are heavy emotions. They are also called negative emotions. There are plenty of issues at the end of life that will require cooperation, support, and decisive actions. Expand the family and you expand the issues.

I will accept the fact that you either have experienced some of these situations first hand or that you know of someone else who has. There is no need to focus on the frustrations that abound when a family is bringing heavy, negative emotions to all the sadness that naturally comes with a death of a loved one. In no way am I saying that it is only the family who carries in the issues. A person who has habitually faced life in lack and fear will bring more than plenty of the same to their final days. It is not uncommon for families to avoid the dying person just because the anticipated level of drama is more than they are willing or able to accept into their life or for those of their own partner and children.

One example was Lillian. She had agreed that I would come and interview her in her final days. When I do this, I have very limited information, so I knew where to find her, her approximate age, and the fact she probably had very little time remaining. I charged my batteries, packed up my video camera, the release of information allowing me to interview her, and met her at the home where she was living with a friend. Lillian had one son. He supposedly had no contact with her. He somehow was aware that she was dying—yet, he chose to stay away. How could that be? My judgements have no place in the videos, so she didn't see my surprise. That doesn't mean that

I didn't have them, or that I didn't vividly remember having them. How can your only son not come visit you? Isn't this supposed to be the opportunity to make amends? Isn't this when you have a final chance to find understanding, and set aside the hurts long enough to acknowledge the family bonds shared long ago? Wouldn't you want to have a last chance to give or receive a message of love? I guess not--or not always.

This in no way was a sad story. Lillian spoke of her hard-working jobs, the lack in so many parts of her life, and the pains she endured with broken relationships, and nonexistent finances. Then we visited the lessons learned, the survival, the strengths she found, and the happy days. She told many funny stories, she spoke of jobs, of her and a friend hopping slow-moving trains to get to the neighboring town, and finally of touching memories and of her lasting love for her son.

What she offered at the end of our interview was a gift that maybe he will hear someday when his resistance and barriers come down. If he's blessed, he may have a chance to receive the gift she left for him. I hope so. She owned her actions and openly admitted that she was sorry.

She conveyed her regrets in statements filled with love and acknowledgement of remorse. "I know now that what I did was wrong. I know I hurt you and I am so sorry. I love you with all my heart. You have always been the best part of my life, and I am so happy that you are my son. I hope you know that. I wish I could go back to change things and make them better. I hope someday you can forgive me. Know that you meant the world to me. Goodbye."

Can you hear the regret, admission of wrongs, acknowledgement of meaning and expression of love? Someday I hope he will have the chance to watch the video, to see her face and feel her emotions as he hears her message. This is a perfect example of why I do what I do. It brings the gifts of the heart. It provides a bridge of time. It blesses the space between two people who each hold a loving and hurting part of the other. It brings the possible gifts of peace, love, forgiveness, and healing. Hopefully, it may bring closure to each of them. When hearts are left broken, the pain can continue to spread and impact others.

Hope comes through the choice of sharing gratitude and appreciation. What Lillian did was an example of her stepping into her power to honor her past and what it held. She recognized that it was what it was. That's the healing part of acceptance. She couldn't undo it, she didn't blame anyone else for her circumstances, and she did not deny that it happened. She then decided to tell her stories from a nurturing heart and candid state of mind. She asked for what she wanted. She trusted that she would receive it and was relieved to know that the possibilities existed for her son to release pain and hurt in order to have a better future.

My role was to bless the space and hold the energy for something exciting to happen during our time together. My questions were asked in ways to bring the lessons out of the low points of life and to seek out and capture the best of possibilities flowing out with her answers.

We create our realities based upon our thoughts, words, and actions. On this day, Lillian allowed me to assist her in creating a beautiful, touching reality in the form of a gift, wrapped in her gratitude and appreciation.

CHAPTER THREE

HONEST COMMUNICATION

Sometimes communication can involve very minor situations. My son had been away from home for years before I heard how much he had always hated having his bedroom in the basement. And I didn't hear it from him; but instead from his wife, who he had told of his displeasure when he said none of their children would ever sleep in the basement. Now, mind you, I didn't think that was such a bad thing. I grew up in a large, farm family, where the children shared two-bedrooms: one for the girls and one for the boys. I'm quite sure I would've been thrilled just to have my own bedroom. I do recall appreciating that those bedrooms were in the basement where it was extra cool during the summertime and toasty warm during the wintertime.

Though in hindsight, I understand how being alone at night in the dark could have made it seem even scarier to him whenever the furnace kicked in or when the house offered some other clanking noises. Though this may not seem like a big deal, it obviously was to him; and yet, it wasn't something he shared during those years. Had he shared those concerns or fears, a change could have been made while it still mattered.

Not having any brothers, he did not have to share his bedroom. From a parent perspective, it seemed to be a childhood luxury that when his friends came to play or to spend the night, the pool table and all of his games were located in the basement next to his bedroom. I was wrong. My beliefs led to choices, which created a situation we never discussed. Had I been more perceptive or had he felt comfortable in discussing it, his bedroom would have been upstairs. Instead of thinking he was appreciating the privacy of his own room, I would've known how the misunderstanding created his childhood beliefs that have lasted well into adulthood.

Some misunderstandings develop into huge conflicts resulting in families that become separated for their remaining years. Thoughts, emotions, and beliefs all impact our behaviors and it is not unusual for anger and fear to rule the day when emotions go sour. An impending death offers us the opportunity to get clear with our priorities.

If there's a past hurt or unresolved issue that has resulted in bitterness, rejection, or even the feeling of being neglected, this is a good time to address those feelings with a parent. Though it may not be easy, or because we may feel guilty for bringing up the past at this time; addressing the issue in our most loving, direct, and honest way may, surprisingly, bring a good result. The same issue may likely be on the mind of our parent but they don't know how to address it either. They may not want to risk adding more pain, or worse yet, driving a bigger wedge between them and us.

A Direct Talking Technique

When we set our intention to address an issue during these conversations, we will want to do it in a way that is loving, but clearly one that is seeking to more fully understand the situation that initially created the pain. This may allow them to say they're sorry. Our elderly generation has not always been really good at expressing emotions. Many of them have survived only because they've learned to become stoic and put their hard times behind them. They did not dwell on their emotions. They may have seen emotions as a sign of weakness. If nothing else, it is important for us to use our knowledge and time wisely to decide what needs to be said, along with what issues or hurts we can finally drop. Because we realize they no longer matter, those are things we can now release.

If you decide to address an issue, here's a helpful hint I learned at one of my leadership classes. It may have a technical name, however, I call it the Direct Talking Technique. This method is designed to avoid judgment and blame, because it focuses only on what happened and how it made you feel. Simply state, "When you did or said this (identify situation), I felt (state how you felt)." Period. And then stop (yup, just shut up and allow the other person to absorb your statement). By using this technique, you are identifying the issue, your feelings, and allowing room for them to digest the issue from your perspective.

The nice thing about this technique is that it works effectively, because it presents the situation in a neutral manner. No one can argue with how we felt. We own our feelings. Initially, they may feel that we are blaming or judging them; but if we simply repeat the statement over, it will be clear that we are just identifying how their actions impacted us. This is the time to remind yourself not to revert to blaming, shaming, or judging.

There is a second part to the above technique for those of us who want to transmute the hurt and add healing to the situation. At the end of the statement, we add the words "—and here is what I choose to do in order to shift this into a positive experience for me-- and hopefully for you (state what it is that you've decided or chosen to do)." Again, you are owning and controlling your emotions and your behaviors. What they choose to do, or not to do, is out of your control.

Sometimes being able to say, "I'm afraid," is a huge step. Fear creeps in from every corner and, left unattended, it can grow and become almost paralyzing. Avoiding the discussion does not make fear go away. Acknowledging fear allows us to talk about it and thereby also realize that addressing it is the best way to neutralize it. If your parent does not bring it up, you may want to approach it with a simple question. Are you scared? Regardless of how they answer, it puts the topic on the table to be addressed.

If we are afraid, it may be helpful to open a conversation by telling them that we are afraid: *I'm afraid of losing you, I'm afraid of living without you, I'm afraid you may be in pain, I'm afraid my children may not know you, I'm afraid of the medical bills, I'm afraid that Dad (or Mother) may be lost without you*, or whatever else may be bringing you fear. And if fear seems to be a heavy word, we can always change it and say, *I'm worried, I'm concerned*, or something that doesn't seem as daunting. The key is to open the conversation and to be willing to listen and receive whatever follows.

Interestingly, the majority of the people that I have interviewed and asked whether or not they were afraid, said they were not. Maybe it's because, by the time I interviewed them, they had already had time to come to terms with their death and whatever it is they expected to follow. I've been told that two specific groups of people who seem to have higher levels of fear as they approach death are servicemen and nuns. I have nothing to substantiate this; however, here's the logic that I was given. The World War II infantrymen (and likely other servicemen and women), who were fortunate enough to survive and return home, buried all of those emotions of fear and dying and being in foxholes, as they came back home, to focus on careers and their families. Now that they're approaching death, those old buried emotions come rushing back to the surface, only to be very real all over again.

And the story is different with the nuns who have concerns approaching death. It is easy to realize how nuns can create an unrealistic expectation for their lives. They raise the bar so high that it's almost impossible for them to be good enough, or to have done all that they were expected to do, or they become very critical of themselves in areas where they may have fallen short in life. These expectations, along with their self-critical evaluations, whether valid or not, are likely to come packed with judgment and fear.

SECTION TWO

I LOVE YOU

Patient of Today

I do not even know you;
yet, tears come during this time.

I may be your love, your child,
your friend, or your parent.

I come to "be" with you. I may
bring peace or comfort, I may bring memories,
or I may bring relief to those who have
journeyed so far alongside you. Mostly, I bring nothing.

I close my life during our time. My worries and work
will still be home when I return. I set aside chores, family,
friends, ballgames, tv time with my spouse, reading time,
or maybe some of my cuddling time.

It's okay because we both know you are
about to make an amazing transition.
You are going to a space of pure energized
Love, peace and goodness where your
loved ones are waiting.

I wait too–mainly
because you should not be alone.
I will be the one you leave behind.

It's all good because I know someone, somewhere
Must somehow love you.

Right?

-Janet Bieschke

CHAPTER FOUR

HOW TO ADJUST TO YOUR NEW REALITY

Highlights was the name of the children's magazine first published in the late 1940s and featured a strip based upon two contrasting boys. Though the magazine attempted to make one boy all good while the other was all bad, the focus was really on the choices each of them made and the corresponding outcomes they created.

Approaching death is a time when emotions can be raw for everyone and the many choices that must be made, though well intended, can easily be wrongly interpreted and may quickly divide us and other family members into someone who is either all good or all bad. This is unfortunate, but sadly happens too many times and creates too much hurt.

Most of the time, we like to view ourselves as good people making loving choices in the best way we know how for this loved one that we are about to lose. Situations may arise that frustrate us, confuse us, irritate us, and leave us feeling that we have no choice but to be strong and clear in communicating or doing what we think is best. It may be helpful to remember that siblings and other family members, including your parents, are doing the very same thing.

When our reality shifts, it is helpful to realize there is always an opportunity to impact the outcome based upon the choice we make. Though it may not seem like it at the time, and especially if we are being pulled back into a dysfunctional family, we always have choices.

In his 1959 book *Man's Search for Meaning* (Beacon Press, ISBN: 9780807014295), Viktor E. Frankl speaks of our last freedom to choose being the choice of how we react to our circumstances. Here are a couple of his quotes:

"When we are no longer able to change a situation, we are challenged to change ourselves."

"Everything can be taken from a man but one thing: the last of the human freedoms—to choose one's attitude in any given set of circumstances, to choose one's own way."

This is so helpful to remember as we attempt to take care of ourselves, our parents, and possibly many others as we navigate through some uncertain times that certainly lie ahead of us. Each situation is uniquely different, even though many choices are based upon common situations. This will be a time when control issues come into play. Strong-willed parents will not want a child of any age advising them on what to do, when and how to do it, or even if to do it. In their mind, they are the parent and we are the child. Period.

Even though I talk about self-care in terms of advising you to take care of yourself, it really needs to be a directive. Take good care of yourself! You are most helpful to others when you are grounded, rested, well nourished, and in good spirits, seeking the best outcome possible for your parent. Because it is so critical, I will address this as a separate issue later in the book.

This is an appropriate time for self-reflection, to sincerely ask some questions of ourselves. You could begin by contemplating some of these. You do not need to share the answers with anyone, but by obtaining some sincere clarity, you will be in a better place to address the issues that are likely to arise. So, what is it that you want?

- Their money?
- Their stuff?
- Time with them?
- Not to have to deal with their issues?
- Resolution to old hurts and unresolved misunderstandings?
- To extend their life so that you can make new memories with them and you and your family?
- Time to tell them that you love them?
- An opportunity to ask for forgiveness or to clarify an issue that happened between the two of you?

It may be helpful to take some time and reflect upon the many thoughts going through your mind right now. Then you can decide what is realistic to happen in these final days and what would be the best way for you to help create them. And what things will you need to let go of, because they're never going to happen, except in your mind?

The reality for so many of us is that we still carry hopes and dreams and expectations while time continues to run out. It's okay. It happens to most of us. I live two states away from where I grew up. Over the years, I would often notice mothers and daughters together enjoying coffee and conversation while reminiscing about how nice that would be to do the same with my mother. I carried those desires in my head and allowed them to manifest as regrets that I didn't live closer.

The reality was much different. Because, even when I was together with my mother, her concerns remained focused on the few siblings that were having issues with alcohol or their messed-up lives. It never felt as though she could give me her time, attention, or presence. At some point in my life, I accepted this and stopped hoping for something that I knew would never come. I realize that she loved me, but that her focus would always remain with those who needed her most. Though I wanted more from her, I didn't need her. Once I realized that she equated needing her with loving her, it made sense.

At that point, I learned to accept her and love her exactly as she was--a mama bear protecting the cubs who needed her. You may have something similar that helps you to realize that we don't always get the perfect life, the perfect relationships, or the ideal situations. Most people don't. And yet we can learn to make the best of it and to be gentle with ourselves and others.

Gentleness is something that I did not possess. As the oldest daughter in a large farm family, my mother expected me to take control of many situations that should have been controlled by a parent. Ultimately, she nicely prepared me for a career of management and executive decision-making. It was easy to make decisions as they affected me, our family, our community, and the many employees within the organization. The longer I worked in administrative, operational, management and bureaucratic roles, the easier it was to focus upon achieving the bottom line by managing the logistics of deadlines, quality, and results.

What she did not prepare me for was being gentle with myself. I did not know how to do that. I was my worst critic in every way possible. Personally, and professionally, I was demanding in my expectations. I expected the best and I worked hard to achieve it. Though I excelled in many areas and received numerous awards and accolades, I failed miserably in being gentle with myself and my family. And to love myself? That came much later in life when I began to do my own homework. And Christy Whitman calls homework, "the work that takes us home." I like that.

There was a heavy price to pay for doing what I thought needed to be done to survive. The biggest one was emotional desolation. The result of my choices led me to a life where I put up many walls of protection in order not to be hurt. As a child with many adult responsibilities, I did not learn to play, to have fun, or to enjoy life. I learned to get results and consistent outcomes. I learned to make judgements and to be judged, all things that provided me opportunity for more 'homework' later in my life.

My world expanded, I created many opportunities, and learned many lessons. It wasn't until I became certified to teach and facilitate Stephen Covey's many courses on effectiveness *(www.franklincovey.com/)* that emotions found a place in my life. And as scary as it seemed, I learned to recognize, feel, and trust my emotions. I had always known *what I thought*. Now it became possible to know *what I felt*. Those are two very different things and lead in very different directions.

Fortunately, as I was coming to the end of my career, I still had time to incorporate emotions as I was trained in HeartMath *(www.heartmath.org/)* and in Appreciative Inquiry *(www.centerforappreciativeinquiry.net)*. In both of these, appreciation is so deeply integrated that the initial questions are asked with the anticipation of a positive outcome. Normally, we look for what is wrong, what else will possibly go wrong, and who will be the one to screw it up and make it go wrong. This happens in organizations and families. It sounds easy, yet it took a consistent focus to change the results by changing the questions. Appreciation and gratitude are tremendously powerful tools, yet, it's also easy to discount the value we will get in results if we are fooled into thinking it's just fluff. It works.

When we begin our day with gratitude, somehow the day flows better. In coaching, we almost always begin with appreciation and gratitude journaling. These are simple and powerful ways to set the day in motion by sending out the type (positive) of vibration that you want. Life reflects back these vibrations in the form of results and they always match. So, when we begin the day with grumbles and complaining, it won't take long before things begin to go wrong and the day seems to add one issue to another, until it all slowly comes apart and continues to flow downhill. To say more about vibrational energy in its simplest form, I'll break it into four steps:

1. Awareness: we notice the results of our life and pay attention to both the positive and negative that we receive. Think of your situations in your health, finances, relationships, career, and emotions.
2. Activate the energy: this vibration of energy that we send out will be either positive or negative. Our choice of words and language are powerful energy activators. Our thoughts, intentional and unintentional, are also powerful means of activating our vibrations.
3. Similar to the reflection in a mirror, life responds to this energy in direct response to what is activated by us.
4. As a result, we then get more of what we were vibrating. This remains true whether it is positive or negative.

So, when we begin our day in anger and worry, we are sending those vibrations out to the universe to send right back to us. The good news is that conversely, when we begin our day in choosing to appreciate and be grateful, our day will multiply and send those types of things back to us. When we become diligent in making our day a choice and a habit, this becomes a wonderful life skill to manage our days. This is a softer skill, but also a life-changer in so many ways.

So, this change in softer skills that led to even better results intrigued me so much that it became the foundation for the case study in my doctorate dissertation[1]. In many ways, these changes in my thinking and feeling processes propelled my life into a whole new chapter. It is the reason so many people benefit from working with life coaches.

By finding my gentler inquisitive side, I learned to reach deeper and find gifts in ordinary things. I discovered patience and what happens when we take the time to bless the space in which we live, to create the opportunities to make memories, and to appreciate both people and things in new ways. It's what made all the difference in the way I show up in my own life, and in the way that I have learned to BE with others.

This was the time when I turned my own world upside down. And it began with the honesty required to acknowledge shortcomings. In being honest and direct with myself, it became possible to engage openly with others—especially those in the final days— without judgment, without expectation, and yet honest enough to be direct and ask pertinent questions in ways that elicited some very delightful, meaningful responses.

---

1   Bieschke, J. M. (2004). *Transgenerational Transference of Organizational Values*, Culver City, CA: Pepperdine University.

A Conversation Filled with Healing Possibilities

One of the many gifts in the final days comes through this deeper level of honesty. For some it becomes a time to openly address old, unfinished business. In conversations with friends, some tell me that they disagree that negative topics should be addressed during the final days. Maybe they are right in that thinking. However, what if this is the conversation that holds the closure or the healing for you or for your loved one? Yes, it may take some guts to be honest with a parent (or conversely from the parent) and say, "When you did (this), I felt (this)," and, "that hurt," or, "I never understood why," or even, "I really need to hear (this) from you," knowing that it's now or never. Because, if not now, when?

Though it may be very uncomfortable, it may also be extremely rewarding to hear what your heart has waited so long to hear. The healing opportunities within the final days are tremendous, but they can easily disappear if no one asks for what they need. After a lifetime of avoiding certain topics, it may take some courage to be honest with yourself and know that it's okay to ask for what you need. We may be pleasantly surprised to realize how much the other person appreciated the opportunity to say what needed to be said. There is so much healing in these direct and honest conversations. It may be the best conversation we almost never had.

People react differently, and we may have preconceived ideas about death and the dying process. These come from our experiences and what we've read or been told. What if they are only one way of approaching it? What if we could build upon the Celebration of Life choices that are beginning to replace the morbid, scary angst of the past ceremonies for too many? I have a friend, Sherry, who has made a business out of turning everyday moments into beautiful, festive, life celebrations, and if that is something you are interested in doing, she gave me permission to share her website information: *http://www. simplycelebrate.net*. What if the final days were like the frosting on the cake and the best part for many was the final part to be added?

Our expectations play a major part in creating the reality that we desire. Again, choice becomes a big factor and it's even better when we see the final days as final opportunities in our life for us and our loved one. How much better would it be for our parent or loved one if we could ease their fears, help them release some of their strongest regrets, relive some of their joys, or to help them see how their life mattered?

Not everyone will share the same expectations and that's okay. It's understandable that experiences and choices lead each of us to our present moments. That includes the fears and concerns that we bring with us. It can also include the helpfulness, joyfulness, and meaningfulness that we are able to introduce into these moments. If you've ever been in a room, a party, or a meeting where the energy is low and dragging and, suddenly, someone comes in with a burst of high vibrations, with smiles and engaging stories, you quickly realize that person was somehow contagious. Soon all the conversations are taking a twist, there are more smiles, increased levels of engaging, and it feels that the whole room has transformed. This is what I mean. There are times for sadness. There may be many times when you're overcome with grief. That's expected. The key is to allow enough space to accept whatever emotions surface.

CHAPTER FIVE

TIME FOR ENGAGEMENT

This can be time for engagement in new ways. Siblings may be making the decisions once made by a parent. I do not know of many parents who are ready to change roles with a child — even if that child is a fully-functioning mature adult. When it came time for my mother to delegate any of her responsibilities, it was strongly resisted. "You're not the boss of me," or, "I've always taken care of myself and I don't need anyone to do it for me." Realistically, when I think about how I may react in a similar situation, I'm not so sure that I would do it any differently.

Hopefully, your parent has already completed some basic advance care planning. If so, then you know what kind of care they want to receive if they become unable to speak. But it's still not enough to cover every decision. This is unfamiliar territory. Here are some things to consider:

47

- Who's going to be in charge of where mom or dad spend their last days?
- Who is going to handle the finances?
- How will the decisions be made?
- Who can be trusted? What happens when they are not acting in the best interest of the parent? How will you know?
- How is the best way to communicate with other family members, with neighbors, with relatives, with medical staff, with caregivers, with lawyers, with funeral directors, with the church?
- Who may need to move in with mom and dad? What happens when they're not wanted there?
- Who deals with the bank and the other finances? Who pays the bills?
- Who handles the mail?
- What happens when trust is low?
- And, oh, so many other things that you may not have been prepared to handle.

The more of the above decisions that are made earlier in the life process, the easier it will become during the final days. Hopefully the final days can become full of space for just being together, treasuring whatever amount of time that remains, time for music, time for spiritual thoughts or conversations, time for nothing but just being together and relishing the moments. This assumes that your family and parents have had the time and the courage to tackle the conversations during some of the good days. We all have our pride, and it's not easy losing our independence and freedoms that we've enjoyed for years.

I learned too many of the above only by being involved with our mother's decisions. Another colleague of mine, Jane Duncan Rogers, has done a lot of work regarding end of life conversations. She also learned by experience. Graciously, she shared her knowledge in her book, *Before I Go, The Essential Guide of Creating a Good End of Life Plan* (Findhorn Press. ISBN: 9781844097500). This is a practical guide to end-of-life matters and is filled with questions, exercises, downloads to assist readers to make well-informed decisions. She understands the importance of having conversations of value. Her website can be found at *www.beforeigosolutions.com*.

Who will be there? Death and the period leading up to death can be difficult for families who begin with the best of relationships. Reality is that seldom are families built upon the old Norman Rockwell images where it seemed that we all got along. Most of us are lucky if we survive the first couple of decades within the confines of family without too many lifelong scars. There's no sense in wading through all of the ways families can fall apart. It's probably safer to say that those of us who are born into great loving homes where parents figure out how to communicate, to set realistic and workable boundaries, and figure out how to add the type of glue that holds family members in love for lifetimes are the exceptions. Maybe life is designed to create enough friction to challenge us to leave the original family and find our independence in ways that better serve our personalities as we mature.

Regardless of the family situation, death will likely intensify the relationships that are already in place. If that's the case, then it is helpful to take the time to decide how to best engage with each other early in the process. This may mean finding schedules for assisting the parents, choosing which person may be most effective with certain tasks, or realizing that there will be days when everyone needs to agree to avoid certain volatile conversations or topics. This may involve setting boundaries and having space and codes set to signal that one of you is extra tired or stressed and this isn't the day for pushing buttons with each other as siblings—or even with a parent. They also may need more space or alone time when their energy is depleted.

We think we will know when we need help. That's not always the case. If we are the one needing help, we deny it. We don't want to believe it, so we don't. Most times, we just do not understand what changes others are noticing in our behaviors, our decision-making abilities, or even in our capacity of doing the daily activities. We are going along year after year and day after day, then suddenly unannounced or unexpected, life is totally different. We need outside help but may not realize it. This is true for the one struggling with the change and can also be true for the caregiver. Knowing when to accept help can become a tricky issue.

In our family, I was very proficient with the administrative tasks and legal paperwork. I failed miserably in soothing emotions and feelings. Thankfully, others in the family were much better for those needs. My focus was on obtaining results, completing tasks, and moving on to the next step of whatever needed to be completed. I did not have the capacity to nurture relationships that would linger long after mom had died. In hindsight, this was a huge mistake.

At the time, there were just too many things requiring my attention and energy. Many times, I was told, "Janet, that's just not the way we do things here." I quickly learned that small town communities relied more on friendship and trust than on legalities. In some situations, this is a great way to do business. Yet, it was not unusual to find that friends, family, neighbors, and local businesses cut a lot of corners that sometimes resulted in personal gain.

In mom's case, people with good intentions noticed her confusions, and it was not unusual to see how the rules had been modified. This was most notable in the handling of her finances. According to a local bank staff, she was observed cashing sizable certificates of deposit (CDs) and walking out the bank with a family member who had questionable intentions on more than one occasion. The bank staff did not have the legal ability to intervene. The firm paid to complete her taxes realized that she wasn't able to provide the required forms, so they helped her by estimating her income based upon the history of the farm activities. In some cases, the results were fine and no harm resulted. In other cases, there were more serious repercussions and consequences.

You may think that because your loved one has always been financially responsible, they will certainly know when it's time to involve you in their money affairs. But what if this is gradual and they do not think anything of the messy details of the checkbook that hasn't been balanced for months or years? What if they trust the scammers who call more frequently obtaining personal and financial data? What if the scammers aren't only those strangers at a distance, but possibly the friends, family, or community members who just have more opportunities to gain from the vulnerable age-related confusion in your loved one? What if they are too embarrassed to ask for help? What if by asking for your help, they are afraid that you will become aware of their growing limitations and forgetfulness? Mom called me late one night to tell me that her bank had just called to protect her account. As it was late and I know of no bank that makes late night calls to customers, I asked more questions about the call. I realized that when the caller asked her to read off the routing numbers at the bottom of her checks, she easily gave them all the information they wanted. Only when I asked who it was that called her, did she admit she didn't know. She knew everyone at her local bank. I think she was a little shaken to realize how easily she gave out her financial information to a stranger. I requested that she immediately contact her banker in the morning and explain what happened, so they could close the account and monitor things for her. Later, I learned instead of waiting until morning, she hung up the phone with me and immediately called her banker at his home. It was 11:00 pm! There are some advantages of small towns where everyone knows everyone else.

I understand the hesitancy of admitting mistakes like the above. The more they share, the more they risk that this knowledge will bring changes. This may include changes that they will not want. One of the natural fears is that their freedom will be taken away. None of us want to lose our ability to make choices about our lives. That's understandable.

But when is it time? When we see increasing struggles in those people around us, we allow them to happen because it doesn't seem like our place to get involved or to intervene. No one intervened when the local church convinced Mom to change her will. By the time I became involved as one of her legal guardians, it became impossible to get the church out of her will. Their lawyers made it extremely clear that even though I had legal authority to act, the will would not change without a lengthy legal battle. They were right. If I were to offer you any advice, it would be to have knowledge of your parents' medical and financial issues. And that includes day-to-day knowledge of how they live.

Parents will seldom admit they are unsafe in their own home. It's their comfort zone and it's where they expect to stay for the remainder of their life. They will likely need someone else to notice when their home becomes a risky place to stay. They will not want to hear it, they will not believe it when they do, and they may resist your efforts to make this type of change. If we are lucky, our parent(s) will make a decision early to leave the place they call home and move into a safer facility or community where others are available to assist as needed.

The other thing that can oftentimes become a blessing is that, by the time we are aware a change is needed, their memory and confusion is at a state where they will quickly adjust to a new living location.

Loved ones and parents expect their family will take care of them if needed; however, that doesn't mean they will accept our help gracefully when it's time. Nor does it mean that there will be anyone available to take care of them. By this time, adult children are busy with careers, families of their own, and are not always geographically close enough to provide the day to day care needed. Some choose to relocate back home, but even that comes with putting lives, plans, and possibly relationships, on hold. There are many gifts within this choice, as well as many surprises. These are decisions that require planning and hopefully, support from others.

The time preceding and immediately following major medical visits, procedures, or physical changes (out of their home, assisted living, hospital, or hospice) are ripe for fears to creep into the space. Knowing your parent or loved one and whether they need this time to be alone or if they prefer to be surrounded by family is helpful to know. The more you understand about their concerns, worries, beliefs and values, the more you can create the type of helpful environment for them and thus for everyone else who will be present during these times.

For some of us, it's total hands-off time. We avoid the talk of death, we are absent from funeral services, and we may not be able to handle it. Or, we may not feel that we even care enough about the one dying to show up. Life happens.

This may be a good time to address hospice care. We now live in an age where medical technology has the ability to keep us alive well beyond what would have been possible even a decade ago. The question is whether that is a good thing. For some, medical advances in replacing body parts is a wonderful way to extend an active life. When medical procedures are keeping us alive long after it's even practical, just because it can, it brings a whole host of additional decisions to make. These may take us out of our comfort zone and find us debating care issues, such as whether the use of feeding tubes or kidney dialysis are the most helpful things to do. And similar to being connected to a respirator, do you know the unlikely chances of ever being taken off of some medical procedures once they are started? Information is critical at all stages, yet many of us learn the facts only after the decision has been made without it.

Medical and Hospice Care

We continue to change in our understanding about the impact of medications and illness on the dying. A palliative care physician, who is also a patient, recently knowingly spoke of the need for empathy in healthcare. About two minutes into his 2015 TED Talk, he cautioned us with his statement that, "Healthcare was designed with diseases, not people, at its center". *https://www.ted.com/talks/bj_miller_what_really_ matters_at_the_end_of_life.*

Ouch! You do not need to look too far to observe how the elderly seem to be repositories after decades of receiving medication after medication, usually with compounding side effects. At least, I have acquired this opinion from my observations.

When I became responsible for my mother's needs, I was alarmed at the number of medications she had been prescribed and was still taking. With research and conversations with her medical staff, some of the prescriptions were discontinued while the doses were changed on others. With all of the different names associated with the same drug, it was confusing at best to research the medications. It seems there are many generic terms that were interchangeable.

I am not sure how an elderly person with mental cloudiness is able to decide what they should or should not be ingesting in the hopes of feeling better. Maybe they just depend upon their doctor to understand their health and to prescribe accordingly. That's a big gamble. Doctors today are limited in the amount of time that they are able to spend with each patient. This alone almost guarantees misunderstandings of the patient's needs. And a misunderstanding of the patient's needs will likely end up with at least one questionable prescription. This isn't to say that there are many great doctors in our system. It just means that there is a diligence required in requesting and receiving medication. Wrong medications can play havoc with the body and the emotions.

Hospice and hospice care is my idea of a medical miracle, because the whole idea is based upon respecting the one dying and their family, in ways that allow the death to happen in the home or a care facility where the parent may have grown to accept as their own home. My father hated hospitals and did everything he could to avoid them. Given any other choice, he wouldn't step into a nursing home either. He was heard to make a statement about wanting to die with his cows when the good Lord was ready to call him home. Fortunately for him, he had a massive heart attack and was able to die in his home. The very idea of him in a nursing home would have caused him to give up early and to mentally will his death. What is important to your parent? Do you know? It is important and the more you know about the options, the better equipped you are to guide conversations when the time is right.

Hospice allows the nursing staff and volunteers to work with the family to make regular visits to monitor health, fill prescriptions, offer respite to other family caregivers, and educate the whole family regarding what care is practical, helpful, available, and to also guide everyone with decision-making options. The more we gain knowledge, the less we will need to deal with all the issues that create fears from worries and questions that will otherwise fill the voids. This is important. Once you accept hospice care, you enter into contracts regarding the remaining time and when and how they will be present to support you and your family. They teach families what to look for, how to recognize the various stages of decline, and what actions you can take. They also guide you when not to take any action because you may be causing additional discomfort. You will learn to notice signs of withdrawal and disengagement as normal.

In addition to the physical support, hospice workers are well trained to provide emotional support. Their primary concern is directed to the patient; however, I know they are very helpful to most families because most families find the dying process uncomfortable. The less we know, the more we fear. This is normal and can be addressed with timely information. It is not my intention to educate you on the many available resources, but being a hospice volunteer, I see and hear the many little miracle-offerings they bring during these final days. They focus on keeping the patient physically comfortable and emotionally calmed. Depending upon their resources, many hospice organizations use volunteers to offer so many additional services that are intended to make beautiful memories during the end-of-life care.

I've heard much appreciation during my own hospice visits. Yet, one of the most touching experiences came from a hospice Registered Nurse whose father was also a hospice patient. About a month after he died, she called to inform me that she was absolutely certain he died with very little restlessness and almost no additional medication because of the experience he had with me interviewing him and capturing his life stories. After I met him and blessed the space we would be using, I set up the video camera and for the next few hours, I listened—and honored his life. He had the opportunity to tell his stories in ways that created meaning as he shared significant experiences. He expressed his love and appreciation to his wife, children and grandchildren. He was full of laughter along the way and it was easy to see how the process brought healing and closure to a life of many years and many experiences. There is something powerful in conversations and the final days are the best times to capture the richness of their beliefs, values, emotions, and everything that adds meaning as they leave a legacy to their loved ones. As a reminder, you must ask for the stories.

You may wonder are you staying because you want to or need to? It may be a little of both. In spite of how you plan the final moments, the parent usually has a part to play. For some, they prefer to be alone and may be in the process of letting go when a son or daughter walks into the room and the parent will come back to the present living space. This may happen several times and may be attributed to one particular child. For whatever reason, the parent has chosen not to die in the presence of the child and they seem to will their body to stay alive until they obtain a moment alone. It is possible that the adult child has been in the room for hours only to find the parent will pass or transition in the minutes that they've stepped out to take a phone call or to use the bathroom facilities. Though it may be disappointing, it is not unusual.

It's possible that parents, who have a lifetime of wanting to shield their children from pain are still doing this type of parenting. This may just be their final way of offering protective care to you. Accept it as a gift because otherwise, you will be tempted to question how they could've done that knowing you've been in the room for hours or days in an effort to be with them in those final minutes.

CHAPTER SIX

HOW TO "BE" WITH THE DYING

In the Joy of Love, https://w2.vatican.va/content/dam/francesco/ pdf/apost_exhortations/documents/papa-francesco_esortazione-ap_20160319_amoris-laetitia_en.pdf, Pope Francis makes this remark: "By thinking that everything is black and white, we sometimes close off the way of grace and of growth, and discourage paths of sanctification which give glory to God. Let us remember that 'a small step, in the midst of great human limitations, can be more pleasing to God than a life which appears outwardly in order, but moves through the day without confronting great difficulties.'"

It's that small step we are called to take. We may find that we are afraid or fearful to be with the person who's dying. Remember that courage isn't being unafraid; it's acting, even though we are afraid. We take the first step and just acknowledge our fears. Then we use this fear to provide ourselves with the energy and the motivation that comes when we acknowledge it and act anyway.

Words are powerful. They give us the ability to bring in information, to listen and to make sense of what we have heard, to ask questions, or to clarify in order to better understand another person. I have learned that the biggest reason most people do not tell their stories or share information is because no one asked them to do so. Asking is powerful.

For almost a decade, I have been capturing stories of the elderly, the sick, and those who know they are close to the end of their life. For them, it's an honor to be asked to tell their stories or to share their history, experiences, and wisdom. It's not unusual for a parent or grandparent to think they don't have anything important to say, any history worthwhile to share, or that there's anyone who is even interested in hearing what they have to say. And yet, every single person that I have witnessed has shared valuable history, unique experiences, and some powerful insights that become a treasure for their families to share. Witnessing is a method of interviewing that is based on Appreciative Inquiry, the universal Laws of Attraction, silence, and very limited questions. It uses an open format of storytelling by the person being seen and heard in order to elicit the best experiences, memories, and history, in order to create a loving legacy for their next-generations.

This is especially true now that we live in an age where conversations have many times morphed into the words we share via our texts, messenger, social media chats and tweets.

This type of communicating is done without eye contact, without reading body language, and many times while we're busy doing other things such as working, making a meal, or attending to other daily tasks.

With this becoming the norm, imagine the importance given—and received—when we actually stop what we are doing, set aside our distractions, make the time, and give someone our undivided attention. What a gift! It sends the message that this is important. It also sends the message that you (parents being interviewed/witnessed) are important enough for me to take the time and give you my undivided attention. That has always been powerful; and is even more-so in our current day and busy time.

Technology has made this process extremely easy, with the addition of very effective video capabilities on cell phones. I encourage everyone who has a parent or loved one still alive to stop, plan to set aside some time, and ask them for their stories. To make this super easy, I've included an easy conversation starter template in Chapter Eleven to get you started. In addition to the starter questions, it is filled with tips and suggestions with the hope that you will be encouraged to use it with a loved one.

We don't always know how to evaluate what we hear. For me, it's even noticing what I'm not hearing, what they are not saying, allowing the silence that comes when I refrain from asking the next question. Many times, this is when their thoughts are carrying them back to revisit a memory and to recapture the essence of that moment, that person, or that event of long ago. It's all part of the process. Silence can become heavy with so many things including their thoughts, memories, ideas, or sometimes just contemplating how they want to answer your questions. One of the more difficult things to do while interviewing or asking questions is to remember the purpose of silence.

When you first begin, it may be helpful to have a few questions written down to ensure you ask them, but also write down a few reminders to yourself for silence, silence, and more silence. While you are thinking of the next question to immediately fill the space, it is most likely that your parent or loved one is still wrapped in the last question. Give that time to incubate, knowing they are going deeper into their thoughts and into their memories and will give you the best responses, if only you can wait for them. Wait. For. Them. You will be glad that you gave them the extra time.

In my role as a personal development coach, we first clarify the desired objectives. Then the goals are broken into short term actions. Accountability happens when my clients make choices to become focused upon taking the next step, and then the next step, and then the next step, until reaching their desired outcomes. The goals are reached by implementing a system of steps. This process is similar. Witnessing or capturing life stories is like driving at night: you don't need to see the whole road in order to keep driving. You only need to see just the immediate bit of illuminated blacktop before you. As long as your headlights are on and functioning, the road will continue to be lit in such a way that you'll be able to keep driving to your destination.

With that same concept, all you need to do is to ask a question and trust the process. Follow it. Listen with the curiosity of a child. Ask another question. Listen. Imagine this is your great-grandparent, or even to consciously lead yourself and imagine yourself as you may have been during that period of time. Mindfully listen. Just maybe…

Maybe –there was nothing much to a question –but the recollection made him reminisce about … a certain emotional resonance, or about some unmet expectations.

I attempt to identify what matters to them and, in the process, I stumble across a fabulous, touching story. It could come from a very particular experience. One question may trigger a completely unrelated experience. This is a piece of uncovering the unknown.

One person said his "strongest reaction" came from song lyrics and a favorite prayer that brought back the nightly family routine. He recalled their mom and the kids kneeling around the furniture to say the rosary and how his dad just kinda mumbled through it. He closed the thought with his realization, "for all the years I was home, I'm not sure he ever actually said the prayers."

Listening in its best form is when you can step into the other's world and see, hear, and understand from their perspective. There is listening that is focused and carefully paying attention to them and their words. There is listening that allows you to listen to their words while choosing which ones you believe based upon your own selected interpretations, understandings and thoughts. There is listening where you appear to be engaged, but you are really only pretending to hear them while your mind is engaged in some other thoughts. And there is just plain ignoring them, which allows someone to be talking to you, but you are not even paying them any attention. The last one sounds quite bad, but I confess there have been times when I'm in the room and someone (usually my husband) is talking to me and the conversation totally went over my head. When caught doing this, I usually laugh and say it's because they hadn't gotten my attention before they began speaking.

When we set our intention to be present and engaged in the first type of listening listed here, we are felt. The other person understands and feels our presence. It's empathic listening and takes our undivided attention. It's powerful listening. It's also communication in a beautiful manner. We cannot do this while scrolling through text messages, online chatting, looking around the room at other people, or stopping to answer a phone call. It requires our undivided time and attention, along with our intention to set aside everything else during this time. Building relationships take time.

An important need for people as they approach death is to find meaning in their life. This is important and critical legacy work. As they look back and reflect, and tell their stories, it's a great opportunity to see how their lives mattered. It's a time to understand they did add value. It's also a time to revisit old stories and maybe to come to the realization that it's time to tell the story from a new perspective. I think one of the biggest ways that we can help someone is to just be with them during the process of finding meaning in their life. What impact did they have? This is also a time for them to share their values, beliefs, and to speak of their dreams, desires, wishes, and hopes for the future.

Maybe you've said all there was to say. Maybe you haven't said much but no words seem appropriate right now. Remember the power of touch. By doing nothing more than placing your hand over theirs, you say enough. Communication isn't all about words. There are many ways to acknowledge each other, and touch is one of the most beautiful ways to express feelings. One situation involving touch happened a few years ago, and I will share it with you to demonstrate the effectiveness of a simple touch.

Wiggling Away

Juanita was in her final days when I first met her son. He was in his early twenties and unfamiliar with what to expect in this stage of approaching death. His mother had lost her voice months earlier and had been communicating using only her pen and notepad. Finally, she lost even that ability to relate to those around her. There are times when it becomes too late to even express the simplest thoughts and needs.

She had her favorite religious compact discs (CDs) playing constantly for her comfort and peace. She was a middle-aged mother leaving a young son to deal with a lot of questions and new experiences. He came into her hospital room while

I was giving her a foot bath using warm towels. Recognizing the awkwardness and discomfort in his behaviors, I explained to him that even though she could no longer speak, she could likely still hear him if he spoke to her. I was finishing up and applying lotion to her feet when I mentioned to him that she likely could also feel his touch and that she seemed to enjoy the foot rubs. I left the room allowing him the time and space to be with her.

It was at about 9pm within the next week when I was driving to be with a different patient that I received a phone call from an unlisted number. I pulled onto the shoulder of the road and took the call. I am not sure how he had my number, but it was the son. I couldn't stop the tears from flowing when he explained that his mother had died and he wanted to thank me. What he then tearfully shared was his experience minutes before her death.

Following my suggestion, he was giving her a foot rub and talking to her when somehow she responded to him.

She wiggled her toes.

That was all.

Nothing more.

Yet, it had meant everything after the many months of silence with no communication. That gesture between them went directly to his heart with a message that communicated she knew he was present and she was telling him, "I love you and goodbye." He was overjoyed that they had been given this moment of connection. He profusely thanked me again, stating that had I not told him, he would have never even thought of giving her a foot rub.

I recognized his initial awkwardness and know that some of us aren't comfortable with just *being* present. We do not know how to handle the quietness, the inability to speak, or feeling that we *should* be doing something. However, even action begins with being present. So my gift to this Mother/Son was to suggest a simple action that allowed him to feel more comfort during his time with his uncommunicative Mom. And without that presence and subsequent action, as simple as it was, she wouldn't have been able to give him the message, nor would he have been able to receive it. It still brings a smile to my heart knowing that their final moments were powerfully special, tender, and ones that were filled with meaning. I was rewarded with hearing the surprise and appreciation in his voice.

There truly are gifts in the final days. Hearing her earlier stories of how her faith had carried her though many obstacles in life, it seemed very fitting that this healing, flowing spiritual energy connected her and her son in their final moments together. It wouldn't alleviate his pain and sorrow, but maybe it cushioned the blow with a little needed relief. To me, this strikes a spiritual cord that radiated through just being present.

I've been told that if a baby is not held, it will die. Maybe we will someday know that touching and holding will also somehow accommodate the release of the spirit from the physical body.

CHAPTER SEVEN

HOW TO MANAGE THE EMOTIONAL ROLLERCOASTER

A normal day in life can be packed with emotions. An imminent death can create many situations that bring even more and even stronger emotions. This is a time to nourish yourself and all of those around you. Some things will be simple to provide, such as placing more filled water pitchers out for hydrating the bodies. It's a small thing; yet, it can bring many benefits to help keeping comfortable. Whether it's the parent, you, or other family members, eat to stay nourished, drink to stay hydrated, and make plenty of room for rest and space available for each of you. Even when naps are not a normal part of life, they can be worthwhile in this time that will be anything except normal for most of you. Take care of yourself as you take care of others.

It's important to find ways to care for yourself so you do not burn out. When you do this, you can care for your parent at a deeper level.

One thing I see and hear is the need for honesty to remain. *Treat me like a person!* Age and health change perceptions of who we are and of how others see us. They also change the way we perceive ourselves. What happened to the person who could get out of bed, through the shower, grab a quick breakfast and be out the door heading off to work within 30 minutes of the alarm ringing? Gone.

A heart attack, stroke, cancer, a serious fall, a vehicle accident, or a host of other conditions can change life overnight. It doesn't matter the age. Circumstances can also change the way others think. Their issues of concern, fear, past experiences may result in changed expectations. There is no doubt that relationships change as the final days come near. Relationships are the lifeblood of our existence. The changes are noticed.

What do we want in relationships? Does it change as death draws near? It's safe to say that dignity, integrity, and respect are always appropriate and naturally welcomed. As body functions shut down due to age or illness, it is not uncommon that uncomfortable realities will surface. A once proud, healthy person may feel extreme apprehension and embarrassment as they find it necessary to accept assistance as they bathe, use bathroom facilities, or with eating. It can be frustrating to have a child be the one who is now offering the assistance. When those parent-child roles become reversed, it takes an abundance of patience for everyone. This is not the role an adult child envisioned, and the initial discomforts can be everywhere and with everyone. Some of the daily tasks bring feelings of intimacy and loving care. There are other things that feel uneasy and are worth the cost of hiring outside help. Bathing is one of those things. Fortunately, there now are more choices for bringing in help for weekly baths, nail care, hair care, and anything that feels uncomfortable for either you or your loved one.

Sometimes it is help with remembering dates, things, and people that is most needed. Dementia and Alzheimer are words that have become too common and have changed the landscape of our times. As the disease progresses, the memory (the age they think they are in their mind) regresses. Short term memory disappears and though they may remember things from years ago, they may not remember if they've eaten breakfast. They may ask the same questions over and over or tell you something six times in a row. Like us, their lives are filled with memories, but they may not be able to retrieve things in context. Senses bring back memories. The aroma of cookies baking may bring back a childhood memory with a time with family. The sight of a doll make cause a grown adult to go pick up 'their baby' and hold it close. It's real to them. A puppy in the room will bring different memories or happiness or fear. We live our life memory by memory. It's tough when that becomes distorted. A helpful child may use labeled photos, memory books, calendars, and conversations to reinforce accuracy of past events, people, or circumstances.

Think how confusing it must be to know what you know, only to have someone who you know well continue to argue with you and adamantly insist that you are wrong. There are times to gently offer reminders of facts. There are other times to let it go. Stop correcting them. When you hear them state things that are not true, their facts are scrambled, and people are misrepresented, just pause.

Consider for a moment that it's truth to them. It's okay if you allow their perception to become the facts for now. When we see two young girls skipping or holding hands, we smile and appreciate their youthful ways. It can help to remind ourselves that if a memory-related disease is playing havoc with our parent, it's okay to just acknowledge that you may be seeing how they engaged in their youth or childhood. If this is the situation you are dealing with, I strongly suggest that you Google or check YouTube for Jolene Brackey, who I've mentioned earlier in this book, and use her experience to guide you. Her material will help you understand that you are not alone. Your parent is not crazy. You are not crazy. There are ways to minimize the pain and confusion. Jolene is an absolute life saver! Her information will help you better understand the perspective and the behaviors of one suffering with dementia or Alzheimer's.

The more you know, the easier you will accept the inevitable behaviors. You may find much humor entwined with the changing behaviors. The sooner you get help, the better this journey will happen. If you are a caregiver dealing with a partner, friend, or other close one, take care of yourself. They can be demanding with the amount of time, energy, and commitment they require. This is not a road you travel alone.

Too many times, it's the exhausted caregiver who may die first because they allowed guilt, responsibility, or other unrealistic expectations to zap them of everything physically, mentally, and emotionally.

Decades ago, that's what families did. Today, there are resources available. Staff in nursing homes and memory-loss facilities are better trained. Check your area to find available resources and use them—for everyone's wellbeing. It sure would have helped our family to better understand what was causing Mom to behave in unusual ways.

Fortunately, we did eventually find the resources, and this made an enormous improvement in the way that we were able to better understand her confusion and her behavior along with the mental bouncing in and out of reality.

Once we could realize that her short-term memory was disappearing, we could better understand why she was talking as though one of us was her sister or her mother. It helped us understand why she hit the man in the stomach after she had repeatedly told him not to come into her room. He also had memory loss and wandered the halls. But in her mind, when he came into her room where she had been visiting with another female resident, he could have easily represented her brother at a much younger age being told to stay out of *the girls'* room. I was appalled to hear that our kind, decent, religious mother hit this man in the stomach with such a vengeance. Mom would never do that! Yet it made total sense that Mom, as a young girl with her sister in her room, could likely have punched a brother who was not allowed to come into their room.

The confusion of knowing and not knowing, of believing something and being told it's wrong, or that you are wrong, must be very irritating. It's a nightmare in so many ways and hopefully, time will reveal better ways of lifting the veil to help us understand how to better navigate dementia and Alzheimer's. It seems to be a nasty disease that causes a person to die piece by piece by piece, over the years. By the time death takes them, there isn't much of them left to be taken from us. The only gift in this type of death is that the family members and close friends have plenty of time to adjust to the coming departure from their lives. Time gives everyone the ability to notice the failing memory and failing abilities to function. The emotional acceptance happens over a period of months, if not years.

CHAPTER EIGHT

BEING INTRODUCED TO DEATH AND DYING: IT IS WHAT IT IS

O' Time, you are a sneaky devil, aren't you?
You are nothing.
You are limiting.
You are consistently inconsistent.
You hold everything.
You hold nothing.
You are everything.
You are nothing again.
Soon even my memory will defy you.
Nothing. Nothing. Nothing.

Janet Bieschke

More than once, I heard about a five or six-year-old child who was sent to go get a grandparent who hadn't appeared for breakfast and come back to the family in the kitchen to announce, "She won't get up," or, "Grandma won't wake up," only to be told, "try again," and then with frustration and a louder voice exclaim, "I tried. Grandma won't wake up!" It was this tone of urgency when an adult would sense that they needed to go to the grandparent.

Most times, these stories are told as though they are reliving the exact moments in time. They speak with the facial expressions visible, the language of the child and the feelings of emotions long remembered.

Sometimes, children were involved when a parent or grandparent died. Suzanne described the bedroom that she shared with a sister. She was the youngest of a large family. Her father had died years earlier leaving the mother with the remaining tasks of single parenting.

She was fifteen years old and her sister had already left the house on that cold winter morning for some sports or band practice at school. She described the normalness of the drafty house with the need to control heating costs and the usual morning chill in the room. When their mother came into the room, Suzanne was still in bed and recalled they were talking when her mother said she was so cold. Suzanne gestured to the heavy quilt tossed on her sister's unmade bed next to hers and suggested that her mother should crawl in to warm up. Mom did, they spoke a short while until Suzanne realized that her Mother was no longer responding. She thought it was because she'd fallen asleep. She was wrong.

She was very wrong and at fifteen years of age, it became her responsibility to make the calls and begin the arrangements. It was a matter-of-fact situation and her story held more facts than emotions. It was what it was, and they had been taught that you do what needs to be done. No one asked how she felt about it; and even if they had, feelings didn't matter. They were tough, hard workers, good at sports, and raised to be stoic in difficult times. You endured, you tolerated, and you did what was expected of you. That's just the way it was.

It seemed to be the same for Patrick when he, also at fifteen years, was accompanying his father as they drove the distance to the paternal grandparents' home. His grandpa had died sometime during the night. That was the morning when he hadn't appeared for breakfast. They knew he was getting older and had less patience for the activities and noise of the grandchildren who, along with their parents, lived in the main house.

The grandfather had cleared out one of his old sheds in the yard and made it into his sleeping sanctuary. With a bed, dresser, and small cabinet, the minimally equipped shed likely provided his much-desired peace and quiet. Patrick said there was no electricity in "Grandpa's house," as he called it, but it did have a kerosene lamp and was in the middle of God's country alongside the old oak tree he had planted years ago. He had built all the buildings on the farm and slept in the shed located not too far from his hand-built corrals, where his animals could be heard.

Patrick and his Dad arrived with grandpa still in bed. The coroner had been called and had arrived, but it was only the driver who showed up. He couldn't remove the body alone. Patrick knew the uncle was grieving in the house and had no plans of helping them do anything. That left the driver and Patrick's father, who stood aside and said, "Pat, grab his feet and help." So he did. He carried his grandfather out of his bed to the awaiting van. When I inquired what he remembered about doing that, he said, "Not much. We carried him out. I remember his feet were cold." That was it. No feelings, no angst, just a kid doing what he was told to do.

Patrick would later be surrounded by death and dying when he was put into the role of killing animals for needed purposes while growing up on the ranch. Sons were expected to step into the roles of their fathers and do what had to be done. He later enlisted in the Army and served as infantry during the Vietnam Conflict. We spoke about some of those years, but he didn't have the details that he still carried from the death of grandpa.

Of course not: Grandpa had called him Kid, took him along in the truck to feed the cows, and he admitted that he believed that as one of the first grandsons, he had always been his grandpa's favorite grandchild. Well Patrick, then who else do you think your grandpa would have chosen to be with him at the end?

Regardless of how we come to learn of death, it is not something to deny. Each and every one of us will die. It does not matter whether we talk about it, think about it, prepare for it, or do anything about it. Death is a reality. It causes much suffering and eats up the majority of the dollars allocated to healthcare. Some of the issues come from our desire to extend life at all costs. Many times, this means we, or our loved ones, will end up dying in a sterile hospital bed surrounded by bright lights, buzzers, and strangers poking and prodding while they do nothing to improve the quality of our life or the ease of our death.

Years ago, we died in homes surrounded by family and friends. We mourned together and found comfort and support within this familiar circle. That's not a normal occurrence today as work demands and individual interests pull families in many directions. Medicare provides more options to have others provide the final care. Children may grow up without being any part of the dying process of a grandparent. Depending upon their age, understanding, and personalities, we need to be respectful of the manner we include them. It is an opportunity for teaching them our ways to understand and make sense of the rituals and conversations surrounding death.

Our children and grandchildren are great observers. They are alert and observant to the moods in the room. They read our body language and know when we are sad. With movies, they are exposed to death. Even if we avoid talking to them about it, they are not immune to the overriding emotional conversations.

Our little ones had many pets. They realized some of these pets would live for years while others would die unexpectedly. They learned of loss and sadness that comes when a pet dies.

Some of our grandchildren go fishing and learn about life and death as a natural process within the food chain. Some enjoy eating deer jerky that comes after hunting season. The life-and-death cycle is learned along the way.

A very young granddaughter was quite sad to realize that the bacon she loved came from pigs. She thought about it for a long time before she decided that she really does love bacon. A daughter-in-law who grew up in the city was visiting relatives on the farm when she almost lost her supper as she realized that her tasty steak came from a very close source. The cycle of life would not be complete if we only acknowledged the half containing birth and growth.

As we grow and experience the cycle, we also experience the behaviors, beliefs, and emotions of the adults in our lives. They help us establish roles and rituals around birth and death. Over the course of time, our experiences will change and grow as healthcare, technology, and social norms continue to evolve. One thing that remains is a need to be supported and to be supportive. And even though we understand the cycle of life, it is quite different when it's a person versus a pet. And it's much different when the person dying is a parent. How do we support the process while we are resisting the impending loss?

A key to becoming the support system they need is learning, understanding, and accepting their desires. You can become a major source of stability in helping your parent make decisions for living their final days in ways that provide some family time for conversations, presence, and hopefully making a few good memories while together. Remember to be more interested in finding the best way, not just in having things your way. As much as you prepare, also allow plenty of room for things to take their own course. Some will not go as you plan. It's okay.

Fortunately, aromatherapy, hand and foot massages, and specific essential oils have found their place in the comforting world. Soothing and comfort for one may be irritating for another. It helps to explore new practices; however, always confirm how it is being received. For some, music is relaxing and meditative while others may find it to be nothing but noise and they find it distracting.

If you already know what soothes your loved one, you are lucky. But remember that changes may come in the final days. What was once a pleasure can switch to something that is no longer appreciated or desired. It's a good time to just pay close attention to their reactions, or just ask if you are uncertain. They will tell you. No matter how much comfort we offer, we do come to accept that a part of life is the end of life.

But maybe we are born knowing that truth. One of our delightful little granddaughters was three years old on the day she was taking a morning walk with her other grandmother. As they walked and talked, the grandmother was very surprised when this little girl looked up at her and matter-of-factly stated, "Grandma Rose, when I die, your mom and two angels are going to come get me." Who knows where that thought came from? But isn't it a beautiful thought to think that someone who already knows and loves us will be there when it is time?

An elderly man spending his final days in the nursing facility surprised his wife when she went to visit him and he excitedly asked her the question, "Who do you think came to visit me this morning?" He proceeded to tell her of a visit from his mother, who was long deceased. He spoke in the present tense and described the visit in detail. His wife could tell it was a positive experience. Later that evening her husband passed away and it gave her some emotional comfort believing that it was his mother who came to get him as he made this transitional journey.

CHAPTER NINE

EMOTIONS

The thoughts, feelings, beliefs, and emotions of everyone can become intense as the final days approach. This is the time where the person approaching death gets almost too much time to reflect upon their past. This is especially true if they've had a lingering disease or their approaching death is simply because of the aging process. As they review the different parts of their life, they will likely bring up regrets. Some will be for things that they've done while others will be for things they wished they had done before time ran out.

Additionally, this is a time for your parent or loved one to receive acknowledgment from those who may have hurt or wronged them. We as children do not always understand what our parents need or want from us. And if we do, it's usually at the time we reached that stage in life where we finally understand what they may have been thinking as a parent. Most times we can just assume that they were trying to do the best they could with the information they had at the time. Most parents of the past were more parents than friends. Many of them felt it was their job to discipline, instill values (usually theirs.), and keep you safe until you left home. And even though the roles of parents have changed drastically within the past few decades, it is easy to see where expectations and realities will always contain some gaps. How do regrets surface?

I'm sorry if I hurt you. I'm sorry for all the times I wasn't there for you. I'm sorry for disappointing you. I'm sorry I wasn't able to spend more time in your life. I'm sorry for ignoring you. I'm sorry for not knowing you the way I could have. It doesn't matter what the issue is, simply saying, "I'm sorry," is many times enough. In certain situations, it may seem necessary to be very specific with the language.

And for some people, it's easier to take the time and reflect before writing out an apology. Later in this book, I have included a specific page in the Letters For Later section that states, "If I've hurt you in any way, this is what I'd like you to know____".

These pages can be recreated and used as many times as needed in hope that they can bring a little more healing into a lot more lives. For everyone who has difficulty saying the words, it may be helpful to take the time and just write them. Surprising things come from something as simple as saying *I'm sorry* to the right people at the right time.

And when is the right time? As in Lillian's story earlier, I can attest to the fact that there are many children in this world who realize one of their parents is dying, and yet they will not come to visit, nor will they call. By accepting our own emotions, it makes it easier to understand others.

Forgiveness: if not addressed, some pains last a lifetime — or more.

Let's talk about the need to say, "I forgive you." Oh, this is a tough one, and for me because it is personal. In my Personal Development Coaching practice, it is necessary that my clients be authentic and to own their stories. But for some of us, it can take a lifetime to clear old stories and issues. You may have some clearing to do, and so may your parents. If that's the case, know that it will be *their* healing work to do. All you will need to do is to allow them the space to tell their stories. In sharing, we heal. Being authentic in this book requires more than a little honest sharing from me. So, with the following story, I share the difficulties that eventually forced me to step out of my hiding places.

Many people are aware of the successes in my life. They know I worked as a Postmaster in several communities, worked on the National Collective Bargaining Team. What an experience! Working in Washington, DC was filled with new information and additional opportunities. I was trained and certified as a Federal Mediator. At the completion of seven months of intense national labor management negotiations where I worked at the main negotiations table, I was called into the Assistant Postmaster General's office. He stated that he was in a position to 'open doors' and inquired where I wanted to go. WOW! I asked if I could have a few minutes to think about it, smiled, and said, "There's a level 20 Postmaster job in the middle of Wisconsin that's calling me." I wanted to go back home to the very job I left. I was homesick even though I had been allowed to commute home once every three weeks. In that manner with family at home, commuting for seven months was tough. Those days didn't provide the technical ability to communicate as easily as we can today.

One of the advantages of working at Headquarters was that I was granted permission to freely use the phone system where I could call home multiple times daily. That was a godsend, but left a lot to be desired. I was so relieved to finish the assignment and to return home where I belonged with the most important people in my life. I was proud of my family and my job.

When I began working for the Postal Service in South Dakota loading and unloading trucks, I presented with only a High School education and a strong desire to work. Moving to Wisconsin later would allow me to return to school during nights and weekends. I had opportunities galore to travel the world, experience new cultures, and learn from some remarkable people. I appreciate and treasure my good fortunes and the successes immensely.

What many do not know is that my successes came at a huge personal expense. Each time a wonderful opportunity presented itself and I decided to accept it, things closer to home would somehow fall apart. I didn't notice some of them as I chose not to see them. I was too busy focusing on the Be, Do, and Have opportunities of the anticipated future successes and what it would mean for our family.

As a family, I was pleased that our children attended parochial school. We were busy with church, school and community activities. In addition to being the Postmaster, I served as the President of the Local Cable TV Regulatory Board, the President of Toastmasters, and a small group of us began a Computer Users Club.

My husband at the time, and I, had lots of friends and were just busy with the many things that young parents do. We enjoyed taking dance lessons along with the time we subsequently went out to practice what we learned. I trusted my husband. He was my best friend and I absolutely loved the way he played with the kids. I grew up in a large family and knew how to clean house, prepare meals, do laundry, discipline, and functionally tend to the needs of raising children based upon my upbringing. I had never learned to play or have fun as a child. I never had time for those emotional things. To this day, I do not have the social graces of knowing how to do some basic things like skate, ride a bike, play tennis, or golf. I am a good worker. Though I have fun in my life, it still takes a concentrated decision to plan for it.

So, with my many successes being public ones, so were my greatest failures as a wife and mother. Yes, I returned back to my local community after the lengthy Headquarters assignment. I was back home, but not to the same home that I'd known. Things were very different, and the damage had occurred in ways that will never be repaired. Trust was gone, faith was shattered, emotions were strong, but they were negative and hurtful.

I was angry, angry, angry. There was more than ample blame to be spread. There were legal issues that needed to be resolved. Our family issues were shared on the front pages of the local newspaper. As our marriage dissolved, our finances dissipated, legal issues increased, the courts were legally involved in our most personal issues, and there were absolutely no support systems in place. Our family fell apart. I tried to manage my sadness until it took its toll. I attended one session and connected very well with a counselor, as she helped me see that I have choices. Sometimes, the most obvious things must come from someone outside ourselves.

When I arrived for our second scheduled session, I was told that my counselor had committed suicide. *What?* She obviously had some personal issues in her relationship. Wow. And I was supposed to be depending upon her to help me figure out things? It didn't take much for me to go home and decide then and there that I would never again take advice from someone who is more screwed up than I am. That became my mantra. It did not help much for issues with trusting. Life seems to always provide us with opportunities and challenges to rethink our issues and expand our possibilities for learning and for growth.

Then came the period of a simmering low-grade depression that, off and on, followed me for years. I covered up the guilt, the hurt, and the shame. I continued to push myself in every area of my life. I had many more successes, but I would never again seek the limelight. I vowed to keep my life private and safe. Every time a nice career opportunity arose, I somehow would sabotage my own chances. I assisted my competitors with valuable information knowing they would likely get the jobs. They did. Time and new choices allowed life to continue.

On the surface, it appeared that I was seeking more responsibility, but inside, I knew that I would never again seek professional advancement if it came at the cost of my children. Never again would I allow my family to be devastated by someone I thought I knew or loved. I became a shell of a person and fought the suicidal demons for too many years. Pride kept me from seeking help. I didn't want anyone to know and no one would ever guess how close I came. Thankfully, I survived. I chose to live for two reasons: my daughter and my son.

The one thing that I needed to do was to forgive. I wouldn't. I couldn't. I didn't. It was hard, hard, hard. I paid the price in my health, my happiness, and my spirit. It was dark, I withdrew, and lived a comfortable life, doing things that should have brought joy. I knew I was just waiting for life to end. Forgiveness? It is necessary. I knew it, I believed it, and yet…

During those crisis years, my son, young at the time, asked me, "Mom, if God can forgive, why can't you?" I responded saying, "I guess God is just better than me." He was wise, but he wasn't the one who had to deal with the shame, guilt, embarrassment and humiliation. Dammit, why couldn't I get past this anguish?

I later completed Advanced Management and Advanced Leadership training. I applied my training in jobs and detailed assignments working as the Manager of Postal Operations, Plant Manager details, and temporarily replacing the Milwaukee District Manager with responsibilities covering the majority of the state. I continued to push myself academically. It was a safe area for my challenges and growth. It took too long for the real deep type of forgiving to come. I learned the payoffs of being stuck in pain. I became comfortable in playing small while knowing that life was calling for me to serve in new ways, to offer light to others in pain, to speak my truth in love, and so many things that could only come after forgiveness was real.

So, when I talk about your need to forgive, trust me in saying that I KNOW it's not easy. Yes, it hurts, and we have our reasons for holding on to our hurts, to someone else's transgressions, to the one who left you emotionally or physically—or both. But the damage of holding onto our hurts, disappointments, pain, and suffering is just more of the same. One of the most loving gifts we can claim for ourself is forgiveness.

It's safe to say that every person I have interviewed had mentioned their regrets. Regrets that hadn't been released hold a mystifying power. Most issues were related to relationships and time. As parents, the way they parented was a usual area holding remorse. There *should have* been more time here or with one particular child who seemed to catch more wrath or discipline than necessary. There *should have* been less time bringing work home into the family time. There *should have* been a better appreciation towards a spouse or partner. One of my wise energy teachers would sometimes offer her guiding statements to remind me of the power in standing in my own energy by statements like, *Don't let anyone Should On you.* Maybe there is a lot to be learned with understanding that.

We all can look back and see where life provided us with the opportunities to expand and learn new ways of being. Some of us needed the opportunity to appear more than once, or in a different manner. If we were lucky, we figured out how to forgive those who we felt aggrieved us. If we were extremely blessed, we figured out how to forgive ourselves in the process.

Not everyone is able to do that during their life. And for many of them, it may be something they want to do before they leave this world. Knowing that death is coming can be a time of life evaluation. We look at where we excelled and where we failed. You may find that you are with a parent who needs to find closure with old unresolved hurts, misunderstandings, and stories. This is a time of opportunity. This is a time of healing. This is a time of restoring love. It does not all need to be analyzed, but it may all need to be said in order to heal and bring closure to a life otherwise well lived. It may not be for everyone, but this can be a time of bringing emotions to the surface.

One of those emotions that is much easier to hear is, "I love you." There are so many ways to express love. In some families, the words flow with ease and on a regular basis. In other families, having a home to live in, food on the table, and a bed to sleep in, were considered sufficient for conveying love. Actions were considered more important than the words. There is no right or wrong way in expressing love. But it hurts to expect it while knowing you'll never receive it.

I have witnessed the satisfaction of a wife who had just heard her husband express his immense appreciation of her and all that she had done over the years to manage their family and their home. Other family members had heard him speak of her in this manner over the years. But somehow, his words had always gone to others in talking about his wife; and she did not hear them directly until they were in the final months of their marriage. It meant a lot to her.

I also had the heartwarming opportunity to witness a 65-year-old father communicate his messages of love and hope to his six-month-old son. This particular father had made many poor life choices that did not have good outcomes. He understood that his son would likely grow up hearing or reading criminal stories about his legacy of these bad choices. His concern was that his son would develop the belief that he came from 'bad stock' and this greatly concerned him. It was a valid concern, for his choice to sell drugs resulted in an overdose and death of another person.

In my work, I am able to help many families create moments that matter. My intent is to bring healing and closure in ways that offer a peaceful passing. In this situation, I asked that the mother of the baby bring the little guy up to his nursing home so that this father could hold his small son in his lap while I interviewed him. This allowed him to speak directly to his son as he shared a story with different possibilities. He spoke at length to his son and he shared the many stories that demonstrated they had come from a family with a long history of making good choices. This man spoke about his parents and his grandparents. He shared their history, values, their acts of kindness, along with stories demonstrating their resilience. As he said, "even though I made some bad choices, it doesn't mean you are stuck with them. You come from a long line of good people." It was important for him to leave this message of hope and understanding to his son who would grow up without his father present. It was pure love. It was giving his son a gift of pride about who he was, and what he could become during his lifetime. It's what most of us want to hear. We are worthy, we are loveable, we are valued. This was a loving legacy.

I do know that it gave this father a great sense of peace to be able to record this message for his son. I later heard from his nurse that it was the center of his conversations during his remaining days. Hearing this warmed my heart. Because we videotaped the session, there will be no doubt of the sincerity and love gifted to the son. I hope they preserve the DVD so that time is erased when he someday views it. He may feel the love of his father connecting their two hearts as he watches that small boy just cooing and giggling as he is snuggled comfortably in his father's arms. Then maybe the words of his dad will sink in at a nice deep level and he will know that he is worthy, he is valuable, and he is loved. That is a gift that can keep on giving. This is also a way of 'holding time' for someone unable to hear a message right now, but hopefully able to receive it at a later date. That's one of the miracles in creating moments that matter for the people that matter while it is still possible.

CHAPTER TEN

DOING WHAT NEEDS TO BE DONE

What can you do? vs. *What can't you do?* (You can't control the other's choices.) This is where many of the coaching concepts come into play. In coaching, my role is to encourage and empower individuals to take charge of their life, incorporate self-care, while they establish desired goals. Once they have that clarity, they are able to identify what challenges and obstacles need to be overcome. In this interactive process, we look for alignment as part of a greater system that brings balance and harmony to their life. Though I've known this for years, I like the way Christy Whitman, founder and CEO of Quantum Success Coaching Academy, *www.christywhitman.com/*, teaches her student coaches to seek alignment first—then momentum. It sounds easy, yet many of us can be off and taking actions before getting clear and aligned. That will often result in undoing, backtracking, or frustrations. As one uncle used to say, "If you don't have it in the head, you'll have it in the feet," and I remember his words during the time I need to go back to retrieve an item because I didn't first stop and think through the situation before taking the actions.

As an experienced life coach, I understand my role of assisting my client to clarify, discover, release, create, and achieve. It is never my role to advise, fix, or to rescue them. That type of help is never helpful. Quantum changes develop at a higher conscious level and require changes from the inside out by engaging clients in a process of question and answers. When we are able to stand in our own power, we find ways to understand more clearly and to create our own solutions.

In this same manner, it is helpful to engage the dying patient in creating solutions to the many issues that arise. It would be a mistake to think there's only one way, that the medical profession has all the answers, or that the patient does not want to be involved in the dialogue. Many times, they can better tell us about their feelings and their needs. They are not less of a person just because they are dying. Remember, we are all dying even though most of us may be pretending that we are not. As I work in my coaching practice, I realize that most people die many deaths. A part of us dies when we are not seen. A part of us dies when our voice is not heard and it feels as though no one is listening, or that our words do not matter to another. A part of us dies when we are not treated as though we are lovable or worthy. When we find our value and our voice, we learn to stand in our power. Then we can take action while in a place of joy, respect, and love. It shows. It makes a difference. It may be helpful to think how we would want to be treated in some of the circumstances or situations that will arise.

In capturing life stories, I have the chance to help the dying say what needs to be said. I want to share another example of what happens in my role of capturing stories, and I think you will find it sweet, sad, and heartfelt. It's what happens when you just show up and allow God to use you in a divinely aligned type of work. I had arranged to interview a hospice patient and he looked as though he was trying with his upmost to fight for each breath. The color of his shirt added to the grayness of his face. Between his heavy spells of serious coughing and with my gag reflex bordering upon kicking in, it was not a good day. He was struggling with his voice and his wife and I agreed that maybe it was already too late for the interview. Fate agreed because when I returned home and viewed the taped video, I noticed something unusual with the audio.

This was the first time it showed up since I had begun interviewing. Yikes. Then I called her and explained that I wouldn't be providing the DVD. It wasn't a high-quality audio, the lighting wasn't the best, and he wasn't having a particularly good day. Having witnessed his condition during my visit, she totally understood. She was very gracious in accepting what I claimed as my failure. I apologized and notified the hospice office.

Two days later, I just awoke when this persistent thought came to me: *If he's still alive, maybe I can go back and do it again.* This was a Thursday and it had been Tuesday afternoon when

I left his house. I wanted to wait until next week, when Easter and all the busyness had passed—but I couldn't. The thought was screaming at me. Later, it was clear that this was Divine intervention.

I called his wife and she said he was having a good day. So we agreed that I would return to their home on that morning. I was ready. He was ready. His wife was ready. Because he was only 40 minutes away and, when I arrived he was ready to do this, he was waiting for me. We all knew that we needed to get this finished. His wife graciously gave me permission to use his name in this book; however, because I never know what consequences may come of that or who in the extended family may take issue with identifying their family, I choose not to share those details. I will say that I could feel the love bursting at the seams of the house as I entered. His daughter was home and his wife was attentive to his needs. As she signed the permission forms, I noticed him in his daybed in the living room. On the wall next him to were crayon colored pictures surrounding him with child printed messages of *I Love Grandpa*. I'd love to share the rest of this touching story. This is only a portion of the interview with him. Being in late stages of a terminal disease, he knew it was time.

The words came slowly and he struggled with some details. He knew he had been married to his wife for over 30 years. She was there. She could prompt him with his memory. It had been 34 years. He spoke of each of their children by name and age. He spoke of his grandparents and the fact they lived long lives. He spoke of the values he inherited from them: strong work ethics and family values. He loved being outdoors, he had goals of living in Alaska or Canada, but ultimately, felt that there was a good reason he stayed here.

He shared the story of meeting his wife. He knew she was the one because everything just felt right. In his hindsight, he explained how he was glad she was the one. In his words, they spoke openly, had no secrets, it's a matter of trust now, and he wanted her to remember that she's the light of his life and he will love her forever. He regretted absolutely nothing about his time with her. He spoke of the unrealness of their first baby and how he was born. They were only a block away from the hospital and how the night before, he'd gone bowling, and returned home, when his parents called.

"I knew I always wanted to be a parent, to be a Dad. I didn't know how much I wanted it."

He spoke of how they raised their sons similar to the ways he was raised. He spoke of his memories and admiration for each of his children. He referred to their second son as a firecracker. He used names, but I switched to identify them by the order of their birth in sharing his story.

"The older son was holding the second son as a new infant when the baby threw up. The older son (still a toddler) yelled and threw the baby. Fortunately, the grandmother was close enough to catch the infant. Whew."

His expressions showed that he could visualize it as though he was watching it play out.

He spoke with a touching deep, deep regret about how he did not spend enough time with one of his sons who didn't show as much love for sports. Fortunately, he realized this error (as he called it) and then spent more time with his next son. He spoke of the admiration he had for each of their sons. Then along came their daughter.

He explained how he was outside shoveling snow when their older son came outside indicating that Mom had news. He was positive that she had news of a pregnancy. He was right. He claimed that he knew by her attitude and the way she was acting. They had three boys, so he recognized the signs. They hoped for a girl to join the boys. Their wish was granted. He spoke of her delivery. He struggled for words but told the details.

He was at work when his wife began hemorrhaging. Instead of the ambulance, he rushed home, scrambled to the hospital where they learned of a condition called Placenta previa. He was frustrated with the amount of paperwork, especially because she had already passed out multiple times. In frustration, he finally picked her up out of her chair and put her in a wheelchair to get her into the emergency room.

"But we got her in there, and they had to do a C-section."

It was apparent how his emotions were flooding through in and showing his face. I could feel them. I could see them. I could hear them. It was here when I asked whether he was scared.

"Oooh yeah, the whole way I was. The whole way. I think we both were. And when baby was born, they couldn't get her to breathe. So, then I had to leave the room. I couldn't stay in there anymore. I had to stand out in the hallway. It was pretty hot in the room to begin with, so when I left the room, I got a little better."

His story was drawing me in and I wanted to hear more of what he was remembering. "So then they put this little girl in your arms and ...?"

"Aww, my arms just melted."

My own heart was melting, seeing the loving light in his eyes as he said it.

"They just melted. There was nothing I could do." He repeated the words as his gaze remained on his now teenage daughter who was present in the room and could hear his words and know his love. "She wrapped me around her little finger and I've been there ever since."

I felt as though I was buoyed in this expansive energetic exchange of raw emotion from a father to his daughter and back again as he expressed love and she received it. It was pure love and there was nothing else to say. This was a time for silence as nothing else could possibly add to what was exchanging between them. I trust that she will relive his gaze and those strong emotions for the rest of her life. How many children receive such a gift? He needed to say it and I'm quite sure she needed to hear it.

After his daughter left to join her cousins for lunch, he continued our interview, only this time his comments were directed to his wife. In wanting to give her a gift that was more intimate as the love between them was so apparent, I asked a very personal question. My question was directed to the time that would likely come soon when she was alone at night and missing him horribly. At that point, what did he want her to know, to feel, to sense?

His gaze remained upon her as he answered the question and shared his feelings of her strength, how very much he loved her—always had—and that she had done so much for him during these past years, and he knew she'd be strong.

I cannot say whether or not she had tears streaming down her face, because I didn't dare look. They sure were flowing down my face as I witnessed his testimony of love to her. The energy was strong and I felt the recording of these words would linger for years even without the recording on a DVD.

They are blessed. Not everyone is. He died two days after the interview was completed. The DVD hadn't even been delivered; but it was easy to know that it will mean so much to his family. My heart felt full of a mix of emotions, both heavy and happy.

Though she later expressed her thanks to me, I was the one honored to step into their lives, their love, and their fears, in a tender way that now is a piece of me. I still vividly see them, hear these stories, and know that the work I do offers value beyond words. In sharing this book, I hope that you as readers, will be inspired to look around in your family, decide to take the time and reach out to ask for the stories that remain hidden in plain view. Ask. It's worth it. I know that the biggest reason people do not share their rich stories is so simple. It's because no one ever asks for them.

CHAPTER ELEVEN

DOING SMALL THINGS WITH GREAT LOVE

Mother Teresa was an inspiration in her words, "not all of us can do great things, but we can do small things with great love." I later learned the quote was paraphrased and misattributed to her. Supposedly her words were, "We cannot do great things on this Earth, only small things with great love" (*https://www.christianquotes.info/images/mother-teresa-quote-small-things-accomplished-with-great-love/*). Either way, I think there's something very loving in asking for a life story from another human being. Because I know how rewarding the story-catching can be, I frequently encourage others to do the same with the ones they value in their life. When I encourage others to interview their loved ones, the first thing they say is,

"I would not know how to start." And though I think it's easy, I realize that the ease comes from the many times I've asked someone to tell me their story.

Over the years, I found a similarity to my coaching sessions. It's not about me! Ever. All I do is hold the space, listen, ask questions, and allow them to do their work. It's always about them and they already know everything they need to know. It's their story to tell. It's their lesson to discover. It's their time to find understanding and meaning. It's their time to release pain and suffering that no longer serves them. It's their healing to receive. And the process always works.

And to help you begin, I've prepared a template that you will find in the back of this book in order for you to begin the process. These questions are only to ignite your thoughts. You will find some of them useful, and you will find that your natural curiosity will give you many more of your own to use, when you begin the interview process. Given the fact that almost every family has at least one person who has a phone with a camera, it is likely that you will be able to capture many amazing stories in short video clips. Find what is comfortable for you and for your loved one, and just begin collecting some loving legacies. Included in the template, you will also find many tips and suggestions that are a result of my discoveries while collecting stories.

"We write to taste life twice,
in the moment and in retrospect."

~Anaïs Nin

It may be helpful to know that one of the most beautiful gifts your family will receive, is the opportunity to hear the stories filled with the history, the values, the hopes and dreams, and the emotional, heartfelt expressions of someone they loved long after that person has left this world. If you have the ability to make that happen now, I invite you to review the template in order to find your inspiration and to take action.

This book resulted from a Memory Booklet project I prepared for a hospice. I had looked at a memory booklet that they had available for patients and asked the question, "Does anyone use this?' It appeared from the shrugs that the answer was, "No, not really."

What follows are the revised statements that are intended to elicit positive memories, and therefore, positive emotions, and a better experience in sharing the memories.

MY LIFE AND TIMES

My name is:

I was born on (date) at (city / state)

My family consists of:

My grandparents:

My parents:

My siblings:

Our children:

Our grandchildren:

Our great grandchildren:

Some of my earliest memories of my grandparents include:

A special memory I have of my parents is:

This is a special story I recall about our family:

In my family, we were taught the value of:

A regular day in my childhood included:

My least favorite chore was:

The part of school that I liked best was:

Here's a quick memory of my youth (birthday, graduation, engagement, wedding, or job):

My favorite (paying) job was:

If I could live over one day in my life, it would have to include:

One person I've respected in my life was _____ because:

When I consider my faith, religion, spirituality, or beliefs, this comes to mind:

The best advice anyone ever gave me was:

One positive thing that I have witnessed in the world was:

A time when I felt most afraid was_____
and here's how I dealt with the fear:

And here's what I've come to learn from some of the rough days of life:

One thing that I'm very appreciative that did happen in my life is:

THE LOVE OF MY LIFE

When I think of the first time I fell in love, I remember:

One of my favorite dates included (dancing, sports, picnic, etc.):

This is how I met my life partner:

The reason I was first attracted to my love is (or what I admired):

A memory that stands out most from our wedding day is:

We have been through a lot together and there have been many things that have enriched our relationship. Here's what I feel strengthened it the most:

One thing that I wish I would've insisted upon doing differently is:

A couple of things that I believe leads to a successful marriage/ relationship include:

THE FUTURE

One thing I'd like people to remember about me is:

There are things in my life that are unfinished, haven't yet found closure, or that I still want done. This is a list of things I want others to complete.

1. _____

2. _____

3. _____

4. _____

5. _____

MY WISHES

If I could have three (3) wishes that I know would come true, they would be:

_____

_____

_____

Letters for Later

The following questions can be replicated on one question per page so that your loved one can complete one or more as they choose. Offer to have copies made of a particular page if they would like to leave those messages for additional people.

When they finish with the letters, just place them in envelopes as appropriate and write the name of the recipient on the envelope.

These letters will be distributed later, on their behalf, as they have directed. They are intended to provide closure in any way that they may like and allow them an opportunity to leave messages for the special people in their life.

Remember, it's their story; so encourage them to tell it any way they want. Hopefully, the following pages will help them bring a bit of closure to a life well lived.

I have also included a special gift for you to use in generating additional communication and engagement between your loved one and their friends, neighbors, visitors, staff, and family. They can use it to let your loved one know how much they matter. It is titled *Notes For You Now*. You may prepare this page, make copies, and give to others (visitors, family, friends) so they can write out comments to your loved one from them. It will be a way for them to give a personal gift to your parent or loved one in the form of their written thoughts and feelings.

The *Notes For You Now* present an opportunity to host a celebration for your loved one. Imagine sending these out to former colleagues, old neighbors, church members, classmates, or relatives living at a distance, and requesting that they complete them and mail them to your loved one. I have found that if you purchase a package of the designed stationery paper and then use your computer to prepare these *Notes For You Now*, it adds a nice dignified or festive touch. It is possible to put all of these questions on one page. I prefer to use the whole page and allow several lines for the response. If you coordinated a celebration-of-life party, similar to a birthday party, your parent or loved one may appreciate having each attending person share some of their written notes aloud. You would have just created a very beautiful and touching memory for everyone present—especially your guest of honor at that celebration. I think it adds another touch to turn on a video and capture the expression of your loved one as they listen to the guests read aloud these messages of appreciation and thankfulness.

You could even bring in a nice decorative basket or container to collect all of the *Notes For You Now*. So many times, loneliness comes in the wee hours of the night and wouldn't it be nice to know that your loved one could have the opportunity to read one or more of the notes just to remember that they are not alone, they are loved, and they do matter? That's a really nice gift to be able to offer someone you love! In the feedback I receive, mostly I hear of how much peace it provided to the person coordinating this life celebration. They had a sense of making a difference where they brought life and fun at a time that otherwise could be somber and sad. What a beautiful gift to give and also to receive.

For the purpose of brevity in this book, I have shortened the space for the replies. In the *Letters for Later* portion, each statement is intended to be on a separate page with multiple lines for the response. I have found that most office stores sell beautiful decorated paper that works nicely for this. A pastel color is also good as long as it is light and not distracting from the words. If you think about it, once they begin writing, they may find that additional people come to mind with whom they would like to communicate a final message. And because these are personal messages, they may be selective in which letters they complete for different people.

It is important that they trust the person who will be keeping these letters on their behalf. Imagine their dismay should they find that the letters were distributed earlier than they had intended or expected? This is an integrity issue. This is a key point.

This simple written act allows them the ability to extend their message beyond their days. I prefer to also prepare these on designed stationery paper. It can make them more professional, elegant, or just more beautiful for the recipient. Remember, they will need room to write, so put only one statement on each page and add double or triple-spaced lines to complete the page. Allow room for a signature at the bottom of each *Letters for Later*.

When I first prepared the *Letters for Later*, I wasn't sure how well they would be received. So, I tested them. The very first person that I shared them with was an elderly hospice patient.

She looked them over, read the statements of each, and asked if she should return the finished letters to me. No, I pointed out the envelopes and explained that when she finished each letter, she could place each one into an envelope, seal it, and put the recipient's name on the front. They were intended to be her private messages to her family members.

I assumed this would be a nice project for her to begin after my visit. I was wrong. She immediately stopped talking with me and almost forgot my presence as she picked up her pen and began writing her *Letters for Later*. I had included a package of envelopes and she was headlong on her mission. I loved knowing that they had meaning for her and they would hopefully be received later by someone valuing the messages written by her hand. It felt significant and rewarding.

Coaching & Capturing
Life Stories

Letters for Later: To_____

If I haven't clearly expressed my feelings for you, here's what I'd like you to know:

Your signature:

Letters for Later: To_____

If I have hurt you in any way, here's what I'd like you to know:

Your signature:

Letters for Later: To_____

One thing that I wish I would have done differently or could do over in my life is:

Your signature:

Letters for Later: To_____

To my partner and love. We've been through both good and bad, but what I treasure and appreciate most about you is:

When you are feeling especially lonely or missing me, here's my special message to you:

Your signature:

Letters for Later: To_____

There will be special days in your life when I will not be there. Know that my loving Divine Spirit will be present, and in case you cannot feel it then, here are my early blessings for your celebrations:

Your signature:

Letters for Later: To_____

When my time comes, this is my way of saying goodbye:

Your signature:

Notes to You Now

To: _____ From_____

A special memory I have of you is:

_____

One thing I've learned from you is:

_____

I appreciate you for being in my life because:

_____

One thing I love about you is:

_____

I want to thank you for:

_____

FIVE EASY CONVERSATION STARTERS
Capture Your Family Member's Stories Before It's Too Late

My tips and questions to get you started on capturing your loving legacy stories.

Invite Versus Telling
1. Remember what it's like when you are told to do something.
2. Be Respectful—always. Invite them to share their stories.
3. Be Curious—even when you've heard this story before.
4. Be Prepared.

Question: What's one of your earliest memories of your grandparents? (a nice way to trigger memories)

Keep It Simple
1. This isn't a test. Talk about things they know.
2. Give them the option of passing over uncomfortable topics. Some things are still personal.
3. Do your homework and know some of the family history.
4. Avoid questions that you know are controversial.

Question: Tell me a little about your parents. Do you know how they met?

Be Interested Versus Nosey

1. If it feels as though you are getting too personal, they may shut down.
2. It's okay to ask about their likes, dislikes, and even loves of the past.
3. Make it feel like a fun conversation and not an interrogation.
4. When the topic turns sad, look for the lesson learned.

Question: Is there anything you wish you would've done differently in life?

Personal Considerations

1. Have a glass of water handy.
2. Have a box of tissues within their reach.
3. Avoid their regular naptime for your interview.
4. Ask if they need anything before you begin (example - toilet break).

Question: What things or which people are most important to you now?

Dreams

1. Avoid judging their life choices.
2. This is a time to ask what life expectations they still hold.
3. It's okay to ask about what they desire for future generations.
4. They may have specific messages for certain individuals here.

Question: If you were given three wishes to make, what would you wish for —and why?

Always thank them for this time. By listening and receiving their life stories, you have also been given a gift. Honor and respect their stories and presence. The very fact that you took the time to invite your parent, grandparent, friend, or other loved one to tell their story sends a huge message. It carries the message *You Are Important and Your Life Matters*.

SECTION THREE

GOODBYE

Soul Speak

I sit here beside your body
knowing you are flying away.

I speak. You do not. Do you hear
my voice or the sound of One greater?

I hold your hands. You are
letting go of my heart. You've released
my hand, my life, our memories—
each of them gone.

Where do you go during these times?
Who are you? What are you doing?
Will you come back? Today? Tomorrow? Ever?
I hold you, I touch you,
I miss you. So very much.

Will you take some of me with you
when you go? Maybe a scent,
maybe a sound of my whisper,
a touch, a glimpse, my heart,
or my whole soul?

For a moment between worlds,
can you stop and give me just
one more hug? Thank you, and God-speed.

~Janet Bieschke

CHAPTER TWELVE

PRESENCE

There are times in life when we do not know what to do, what to say, or even what to think. That is because sometimes there is nothing we can do to change the situation, nothing we can say that will make things better, and our thoughts are scattered because the emotions are bouncing all over the place. We may be sad, scared, fearful, worried, hurt, confused, and even angry about the situation that we are facing. These are the times when it may be helpful to remember that our presence may be enough. Just showing up can speak volumes, just sitting quietly amongst the busyness of others can provide a sense of stability, and just doing nothing can be the most helpful thing possible at a given time.

Yes, there will always be time to take action and to be doing things, but knowing when, where, and how makes all the difference in the world. Wrapped in our nothingness, lies the possibilities of everything: inspired action, helpful thoughts of seeing things differently, and creating space for new opportunities and spiritual guidance to come to us. This gives the ability to be proactive rather than reactive before speaking, doing, or even considering what the next step could be. For some, it may be crawling in bed with another: it may be comfortable to sleep with a parent. For others, it may bring back the comfort of being the child in its real memory of just being in the presence and feeling the togetherness. This is something that either comes naturally or not at all. If the opportunity is there, know that it is a natural action for many. Sometimes, it can be the simplest way of sharing space and allowing your presence to bring peace, stability, and a sense of love to someone who needs it more than you may imagine.

I like to think of being young and having sleep-overs, when some of the best conversations came after the lights were out and we shared stories. Even now, when I attend conferences and women's gatherings, it's common to share a room with a complete stranger. With only one night in the same ship cabin or room, we end up talking into the wee hours when we finally give in to sleep. And many times, the silence of morning wakes us as lifetime friends. There's just something that feels like you're out camping and experiencing the newness of discovering our connections to nature and people.

Presence is not nothing. Presence can be everything. A lovely way to determine how presence will serve us may lie in the question: what is the greatest contribution I can be at this time? Notice that this question allows for no action to also be the answer. *BEing.* Just show up as you are: without judgement, without a need to control anything, and without expectations. It can also be what carries in the emotions of acceptance, love, caring, and hope. This is presence: show up and BE present. That's all, and it's enough.

Presence can be a divine or supernatural spirit felt or the physical act of being present. Or it can be a combination of these. Maybe the first time I became aware of this combined type of presence was when I questioned the 'feeling' hovering over me and the hospice patient beside me. She was in her bed, which had been relocated to the living room, her family had left to attend some event for the afternoon, and I was there to provide the respite relief. She was sleeping, or in a medically relaxed slumber, while I sat quietly in the chair next to her bed. I felt a presence in the immediate vicinity of the room. Yes, a Presence in our presence.

Maybe my thoughts were overly active, or my feelings were overly sensitive, but I became alert to one singular question bouncing through my mind: If the Angel of Death is hovering in this small room, how can he/she/it tell us apart? This was a very real moment for me. In these moments, details matter. Other than her in bed and me in a chair, I didn't see many differences. We both had physical bodies and were located on the same street, same house, and were physically located right next to each other. She was about my age and female. We both had lost the color in our hair. I knew it was almost her time. I was quite sure (hopeful) that it wasn't mine.

I've been in vehicle accidents, risky situations, dangerous locations, and had opportunities over the years if my time was up. Could it be that I'd meet my Maker only because I was sitting in the wrong damn place? Obviously, the system these spiritual energy beings utilize is more discerning and thankfully, I didn't find out the inner workings of the coming-to-get-you identification process that afternoon. And that was just fine with me.

The easiest way to describe presence is to just be there with someone. It sounds easy, yet, it isn't always so easy to do because our expectations and judgements can get in the way. Sometimes, it is the desire to change someone or their circumstances when we think we know what would be best—or at least better—for them. Sometimes we are right, but it doesn't matter because it isn't about us or about our opinions. The simple ability to accept someone 'as is' can be difficult at times. It's more difficult when the person is someone we deeply care about. We may want to fix things, avoid things, or change things that are happening around them. I will share what I have found to be helpful when my life is too busy and hectic and I know that someone else needs my presence. Maybe you will also find it helpful.

Mindfulness Exercise

I sit or lie comfortable. I close my eyes and notice how my breath flows in and out. I don't try to change it in any way. I just notice the rhythm of the breath and try to be present with it. I become aware of the wisdom and love of this soul. I know that it is always there. Sometimes, it feels that it's wrapped up inside my heart and other times, it seems to be in the space all around me. Sometimes, it doesn't feel anyplace close to me and it is quiet or almost hiding. In these times, I use either my thoughts or words and invite that guiding presence to show up in ways that are best for the moment.

I have learned to trust that it's there, hears me, and is always awaiting my call for it to take a larger presence in my life. If I am impatient and looking for a tangible result, I may get nothing. Those are the times I am attempting to control things and allow my ego mind to act up. My impatience will soon become a reminder that it's not about me. Once I ask for my spiritual guides, my divine presence, my higher power, or my soul to assist, she always does! I breathe deeper, slower, and allow myself to trust in her presence and guidance.

I don't always refer to this being as Her or She, because on some days, my years of religious upbringing kick in, and then it's my Father, Lord, or one of the Saints who come forth. This terminology is a 'whatever' for me; but He, She, All-That-Is, or It, is always my Radiant Divine Source. This may be different for each of us and my goal is only to acknowledge the presence that IS with us. Sometimes I ask for specific guidance, and other times I focus on the situation at hand and wait for a message that bubbles up through my thoughts, intuition, or maybe just know and trust that something will come to me when the time is right. All I do is trust and allow, knowing that my Radiant Divine Source always works through me, and sometimes in spite of me.

But once I place my intention on this guidance, ask for the spiritual connection, and attend my focus upon my inner being, then I will simply thank my spiritual being and go about my day. I know that what comes through me will always be for me and for the good of those around me. It may be through my words, my actions, or just in my presence with another. This is a simple, yet powerful practice to learn and apply in life.

Sometimes, I will say something that someone else hears entirely different from what I was thinking and what I thought I'd said. When that happens, I just accept that they heard or felt what they needed to hear, or what was best for them. I love it when that happens because it takes the pressure off me to know what they most need. Again, that's what I call the Presence that lives and works through my presence with another human being. Without having the answers, knowing the issues, or even understanding their needs, I can just show up and serve in ways that become helpful to someone else. You can too.

The situations always allow me to call upon and use my soul gifts. These are a deep sense of being, bringing joy and peace, comfort and assurance, acceptance and trust, understanding, and even light-hearted humor and laughter. The vibrating energy is what connects our hearts and souls. I bless this space between me and my Divine, my patient and their Divine, and the space between us. That covers about everything that will need to be in alignment before we take any type of action, because our Spirit can take control and do everything necessary. These gifts from the Spirit may include forgiveness, release of regrets and not being enough during life, or many expressions of love, trust, acceptance and peace.

Everyone deserves peace of heart and peace of mind. This includes babies, teens, middle-agers and those in transition. A big part of this type of peace comes from mindfulness and presence. There are many ways to bring Presence into our daily lives. The practices of attentive mindfulness along with the learned ability to separate from our thoughts bring in spaciousness and vitality. A few powerful practices include breath awareness, inner body awareness, listening to sound and music, and connecting with nature.

If you want to work with this, try to suspend your own beliefs and trust the other person is exactly where they are intended to be … right here and right now. Trust that they are following the path they chose a lifetime ago. If something appears to conflict with your beliefs or expectations, realize *you* own *those* issues. Your reaction is intended for your growth and expansion. Accept and allow their life to unfold exactly as it is. Trust it to be okay. Look for the good in each situation. Look for the fun or humor that wants to come forth. Set your intention to see the holy light shining upon you, the others, the room, the pets, the staff, and all present. You can invite the spiritual presences into the room. Look for the blessings to surprise you as the day progresses. Ask and you will find them along with their gifts that may arise unexpectedly. Asking can be as simple as blessing the space between you and the others. In doing this, you will become connected to something larger than yourself. The time spent with your loved ones may become more energizing, deeply meaningful, and filled with spiritual experiences.

I was truly blessed when my path crossed with Nic Askew (*www.nicaskew.com*) during a soul-biographies retreat after I'd been interviewing for some years. I learned a different way of interviewing that held no questions. It changed the course of work I was doing and taught me to look for the nothingness. In this, I would find everything needed to reach deeper into the connections with others. I am indebted to him and would like to close this section with something he said that reinforces my truth that this work has the ability to bring peace:

You don't have to fight, there is nowhere to go, it is painfully simple. It takes one inch of courage and a little stillness to say 'I love everything' and then to understand that you can recognize yourself in the reflection of the other ....
then there is peace.

--Nic Askew

CHAPTER THIRTEEN

STORIES LIVE ON

I end with this beginning because it reflects the way life flows. It comes in cycles; and many times, new ways, new choices and ways of living result from the death of our loved ones. As we observe or experience someone's death, it prepares us for our own transition. We ask new questions. Are we ready? Have we done the things we wanted to do? Are we living in alignment? Is there someone who needs to hear something from us? We model and prepare those who follow us on this journey. We look back over experiences. When I look back over this journey, I remember how it began with David, the person whom I mentioned at the beginning of this book. I couldn't have written this book without him.

David

I received a call from the hospice staff. A patient had a friend who was having a difficult time saying goodbye and accepting the fact (patient David) was dying. I was asked to assist him write a letter to his friend. I received the request call on Thursday prior to Easter. We determined that it would be okay to wait until after the Easter holiday, but not too much longer as David wasn't doing real well.

After our Easter brunch at our daughter's home, I asked my husband if he would mind if we drove over to the hospice location so I could meet him (Connection). David was in the dining room and I could barely understand his whispering voice. *Oh my, it's already too late!* After a short time, I then asked hubby if he would mind going to RadioShack, an electronic store, so I could shop for a recording device and a clip-on Microphone.

Somehow the idea of a recording had come to mind and I asked if it would be okay to pursue. I received a Yes from the staff who were able to send over a videographer and a yes from the patient. His daughter objected to the idea of all engagement. He rejected this objection and said this was something he wanted and intended to do.

We agreed I would return the following day at 11am. However, when I arrived shortly before 11, he had just been bathed, dressed, but still hadn't eaten breakfast. Nutrition is important (along with bathroom, meds, water and having tissues available) so he agreed to get breakfast as I arranged the room and my recording equipment (batteries, lighting, and chairs). The clip-on mic was perfect, and I used a headset to ensure that his voice was being captured for whatever pieces of story he would share.

Imagine my surprise when this fragile man told story after story for 90 minutes. Wow! Where did that gust of energy come from? Willpower can kick in with adrenaline and show up in magical ways. He told of being a little boy crawling from his bedroom trailer home window directly into his grandma's adjoining home. Though this time was only for the first 18 months of his life, he spoke as though it was yesterday. The smile spreading across his face told me this was a loving memory.

He talked of the discipline from his father when he, at five years old, ran out into the yard after the bean truck. He had specifically been told not to go near it because his dad didn't want him to get hurt. And of course, right in front of his father, the truck came by, and he went tearing after it, not thinking. He came back with two hands full of the beans, only to have to throw them away. What he recalled most vividly were his dad's words that he would get his discipline the next day. Oh, the agony of the waiting, and he felt so bad because he knew his Dad was trying to teach him right from wrong. The next day, his 'whooping' came, but it was the rough wait that he dwelled upon as his thinking of it had kept him awake much of the night.

He and his older brother would take the boat out frequently for fishing. He got the hook stuck in his hand while they were at a campsite. His Dad whipped out a jackknife, wiped it on his pants, and dug in there until he was able to get the hook out. His memories were very clear and specific. The emotions remained when his brother took him out in the wooden rowboat to an island with turtles. Being a reckless kid, the brother shot and killed a turtle only for both of them to begin crying after they realized the harsh consequences of this action. It couldn't be undone. At five years, he wasn't prepared for the death of the turtle, nor the tears from his older brother. Boys didn't show emotions. Even though he understood that cultural norm and belief, he also understood it was the caring within this brother who read to him, and it was the nurturing side that had helped him learn to both read and write.

Another older brother was the brains and had read almost every book in the library according to David. He spoke of his loving mother who would scream and run if anyone brought a mouse into the house. He continued to relay a wonderful legacy of story after story, providing a rich history for later generations. He shortened some of the stories, but there was no question that his memory was vivid with details. The teeth of a chasing dog at his uncle's place, he thought he would die, and how he came running back to the car with a running leap and made it through the window of the car just in time.

Laughter filled the room as he spoke of his wife. He spoke of the permission granted from her dad for her to date him. Supposedly her first boyfriend did not get her dad's permission, so she broke up with him. He was glad her father approved of him.

He spoke of the birth of each of their children. The smile in his eyes, along with the way he cradled his arms, radiated through me as he described first seeing, touching, and loving each of their babies. He just couldn't get over the fact that his firstborn was just so beautiful. "I looked at her and was just immediately in love with her. Oh my gosh, that's my baby. She was a little girl and she was so cute. She was so adorable, completely adorable."

He described the blueberry eyes of their son and how alert he was as a baby. Compared to the daughter, this son was quiet and took after his mother. Many, many stories followed describing his family, which will be left for their reminiscing. At times, he was in tears, laughing as he told me funny, touching stories.

We spoke of the differing amazing values. He described the time their daughter had given away her last $5, frustrating her mom. Mom later apologized, because she knew where the trait came from (her). How tender and touching were these moments as he relived earlier memories of each of his children including the enormous pain when they lost a child. (Closure and healing.)

As we neared the end of his interview, he shared emotions of losing a grandchild and the enormous pain they felt. In a flash, we moved on and soon he spoke of each grandchild with stories and such pride was held in his messages to each. He included his six-month-old littlest one in this interview and he closed with praise and compliments for each. His wisdom to them came as advice to, "read books as part of your education. Live in the now. Don't worry so much about your past or what may come. Stay involved in life, enjoy it, and remember to be kind to others. Encourage others, use care in choosing your friends. Be happy. Don't judge friends by the cover. I love you and I hope this helps you get through life easier. Don't feel sorry for yourself, no matter what you are facing."

We discussed the happiest moments of his life (personal but filled with loving relationships). I asked him what he wanted to say to those who would later watch this video and what he would like them to know. He was grateful for his friend who inspired this work, the other friends who've been so close (he named them along with expressing his appreciation), his brothers, and the extra attention he is now receiving as he really did need this loving and closeness since he'd been sick. He had no regrets, but apologized to anyone he may have made sad during any part of his life.

He gave advice on the younger generation. "Be strong. Don't feel sorry for yourself or you'll just be sad for nothing. Reach out to people, be supportive, be friendly, don't complain *I'm dying, I'm dying*. That's a bunch of baloney, even when you're dying. You need to live with the living."

I inquired whether or not his thoughts changed since being diagnosed and he shook his head.

"There were periods of darkness for me, but most of my life, I've looked for something to smile about. Always leave people smiling."

He spoke of his God being his closest and strongest light, Savior, and strength.

"It's not how much property I own, how many cars I have in the garage. I believe in Jesus, the afterlife and I believe I'll see all of you again. Don't walk around thinking, *Oh, I have to pull my smile out of my pocket*. It should always be on your face."

He gave his love to each family member again and to each friend that touched his life.

After more funny stories of camping, his cooking of deep fried frog legs, he spoke of his coming opportunity to meet his Savior, his Mother and so many relatives who will be waiting for him. He finished with a big smile for the camera, and again, "I'm sorry if I forgot to mention anyone, but thank you all (more names). I love you all, God bless."

And with another smile and a wave, he closed with, "Goodbye."

Ninety minutes! I was most impressed with the satisfying smile on his face. What began intended as a goodbye for a friend expanded into his loving farewell message to so many. This interview that I thought may be sad and difficult to hear was such a rewarding gift for both of us. I could only imagine how nice it will be for his family to hear his voice as his stories will be heard over and over. His specifics of dates, names, places, conversation details and his strong outbursts of laughter are what I recall all these years later. What a beautiful gift.

Everyone deserves peace of mind, peace of heart, and a peace in passing. By living a life of joy, alignment and rich heartfelt connections, we are able to live with gusto. We write the stories in the moments. We can choose to create moments that matter with the people who matter. We create the life where our stories along the way are full of life. We can tell stories of how we held a little baby so close for so long that we can still feel that heartbeat all these years later, or of how we danced so long that night our knees still hurt.

We can tell stories shared by parents of the little boy who wanted to go outside and play with his chocolate friend and his mama asked him if he was the vanilla friend; the little boy who won the, "my daddy's bigger, my daddy's tougher," argument by stating, "My grandpa has a bigger belly than yours." Or the little five-year-old girl who made an observation that caused both of her parents to laugh when she stated, "I hate being the height of butts."

These are simple, everyday, ordinary moments. They are also moments that bring back a piece of time, a memory of a loved one, a shared connection—a moment that matters with the people who matter. So, when it's our time, we are in peace, as are those we leave behind. That matters! Because of the work I do, people who already understand the value of finding peace of mind and peace of heart, now learn how to create the type peaceful passing for their loved ones in ways that bring healing and closure.

I'm looking for individuals who want to learn how to have the specific conversations and also how to create moments that matter with the people that matter in ways that:

- Uncover things unknown
- express emotions-- both of love and loss
- leave legacies
- release regrets
- and share stories for future generations while doing it in ways that bring healing and closure-- not only for the one passing, but also for the ones left behind.

Who do you know?

I appreciate you for purchasing this book, and I sincerely hope you are blessed with ideas for how to better and more gently spend the final days with your loved one. If I can be of assistance, reach out to me at *www.drjanetb.com*.

CHAPTER FOURTEEN

THE TIME IS NOW. WHAT IS HAPPENING?

Even when it's time, the time can vary for death to occur. It can happen within hours or over the period of days. Families think it's time, come together only to find that now isn't the time. And if this happens on several occasions, it is difficult emotionally as you prepare, receive a reprieve, and prepare again.

There are so many emotional physical and spiritual changes taking place in the final days that it may be helpful to have an idea of what can be expected. There is no format or time schedule of the changes in the dying process, but there are some common patterns. You may have noticed your loved one withdrawing from conversations, losing interest in most activities, or not even responding when someone is speaking to them. They may be speaking to someone you cannot see. Listen without interrupting and you may be pleasantly surprised to hear them talking to someone who has come to get them. In some cases, they seem to be talking to a parent or another person who played a significant role in their earlier life. There's a lot we do not know about this process of dying.

You may notice that your loved one is sleeping more and eating less, or just not responding to you in the same way that they would have before. This is still a time to sit with them, talk to them, hold their hand, and do some of the things in the same way that you would have if they were alert and awake. You might notice that they are less alert than they were before so identify yourself, remind them who you are, and just make statements to clarify what's going on. As their body does not require as much food or drink, keep chips of ice or frozen juice available in lieu of a full glass of fluid. The body no longer needs food in the final days and may have difficulty digesting it even when you are able to convince them to eat it. You may notice loud gurgling sounds from congestion. This is uncomfortable for you to hear; however, this doesn't mean they're in pain. It may help if you just turn their head to the side to assist in removing fluids or secretions.

A lack of oxygen may leave them restless and making uncommon gestures like pulling at their clothing, maybe look like they're reaching for something, or making the same motions over and over. Allow the movements without interference, talk to them, read to them, play music for them if that soothes them, and continue to speak in your normal tone of voice.

You may notice the color of their skin changing or that their extremities feel cold. This is a time when the body focuses its energy on the major organs and may not be getting circulation to hands and feet. I have heard that this does not mean hands and feet are cold and I've also noticed a caregiver covering them with a light blanket. When you don't know what to do, ask the medical staff. They are extremely helpful with sharing information. And it's easy to have questions. Because at the same time you notice cooler hands and feet, your loved one may also be running a fever.

More personal care may be required as bodily functions change. They may need more hygiene care to remain clean and comfortable. In all of this remember there is no right way or wrong way. There is just their way--and it's okay. They may need your permission.

Even when you are not ready to release your loved one, they may say things that seem unusual and out of place. These comments may come as they seek your permission to release them. Their last concerns may be for you and your well-being. They want to know you will be okay after they are no longer with you. If they ask for your permission to let them go, give it to them wrapped in your words of love, appreciation and thanks for your time together, tell them goodbye. Let the tears flow if necessary as it's a natural release of energy and emotions. Do what seems natural without judgement. Some people will crawl into the bed and hold their loved one while others are more comfortable using words to convey feelings. Trust yourself.

Trust yourself in whatever you decide to do but know that you are not alone. Information is available, but only if you go look for it. That means your most relevant information is always being revised and will always be at the tips of your fingers by use of a search engine and the internet. Additionally, I suggest checking out these sites:

http://www.beforeigosolutions.com/, http://www.simplycelebrate. net/, and *www.yourendoflifedoula.com*

Thank You for This Day Lord.
Today I will be present.
I will let go. I will trust.
I will receive total Divine Guidance
As always, it is enough.

Janet

About the Author

Janet is a life coach, author, and inspirational speaker teaching Baby Boomers from around the world the importance of honoring their aging parents and avoiding regrets by capturing as many stories as possible before it's too late.

She and her husband Richard live in rural Wisconsin and are overly-blessed with their beautiful, growing family that blends their six adult children, their spouses, 22 grandchildren and 4 great grandchildren. They enjoy traveling to visit this expanding family, who are now living in six different states.

photographer Stacy Kaat: www.stacykaat.com

Retiring after 34 years in the corporate world, Janet retains a wealth of industry skills: communication, leadership & executive, operations & organization change tools, time management, human resources and finance management.

Since becoming an Appreciation Life Coach in retirement, Janet brings success to those who are ready to make life changes with ease, joy and grace while they obtain their desired Peace of

Heart and Mind. She has mastered the techniques of bringing Peace in Passing to those about to leave this world and to those they leave behind. Her clients are left in tears of appreciation and joy.

Need More Support: Let's Talk

**Complimentary 20-Minute
Consultation with Dr. Janet**

I'm here to help you navigate this time of transition and explore the possibilities of creating Peace in Passing for your loved one.

Please schedule your complimentary consultation using one of these two methods:

www.drjanetb.com/schedule

Contact Me

If you would like to use this book to facilitate book discussions, please do. I'd love to hear about your results, what additional questions arise, or how you utilized this book to further the discussions.

If you use the tools to create a celebration for a loved one, I would be delighted to see your photos and to hear your stories.

If you just want to share your comments about this book, I'd be honored to receive your take-aways and ideas. Thank you.

I may be reached by phone at 1-920-946-7413
By mail at
W6998 COUNTY RD U
PLYMOUTH WI 53073-4537

Or you can reach me on the Facebook Page of Capturing and Celebrating Life Stories: *https://www.facebook.com/drjanetb/*

Finally, if you liked the book and you want to help others find some direction at a critical time in their life, one of the best ways to share this information is to go to *www.drjanetb. com/bookreview* and write a quick review. You will be helping others and I would really appreciate it. Thanks very much!

Manufactured by Amazon.ca
Bolton, ON

10909225R00092